Alex,
Who Won His War

WALKER'S AMERICAN HISTORY SERIES FOR YOUNG PEOPLE

Alex,
Who Won His War

CHESTER AARON

Walker and Company
New York

First published in the United States of America in 1991
by Walker Publishing Company, Inc.

Published simultaneously in Canada by Thomas Allen & Son
Canada, Limited, Markham, Ontario

Library of Congress Cataloging-in-Publication Data
Aaron, Chester.
Alex, who won his war / Chester Aaron.
p.   cm. — (Walker's American history series for young people)
Summary: In the final months of World War II fourteen-year-old Alex, worried about
the fate of his brother fighting in Europe, falls into the hands of two Nazi spies intent
on sabotage.
ISBN 0-8027-8098-9
[1. Spies—Fiction. 2. World War, 1939–1945—United States—
Fiction.]   I. Title.   II. Series.
PZ7.A12A1   1991
[Fic]—dc20   91-446
CIP
AC

Text Design by Georg Brewer

Printed in the United States of America

2   4   6   8   10   9   7   5   3   1

This book is for Benjamin, Molly Rose,
and Kelly Paloma Segal

Alex,
Who Won His War

Alex Kellar
R.F.D. 2
Pequod, Connecticut
December 6, 1944

Sergeant Oliver Kellar
Company B, 4th Bn. 5th Regt.
101st Airborne Div.
A.P.O. 606
U.S. Army

Dear Oliver,
    I won a spelling and writing contest yester-
day. Best in eighth grade. I sure hate these tiny V
letter forms though. You just get started and you
have to stop. Lucy says they get there faster
though and they save paper which helps us win
this war. Olly, I sure miss you. I took the Iris out
yesterday not to fish just to sail her. It was sure
lonesome without you. I went out so far the Coast
Guard hailed me and sent me back because there
were German subs not far out and they could get
in close to where I was sailing the Iris. They sank a
oil frater just last week. Six miles off shore. You
can bet there aren't many fishing boats sailing out
of Mass. or Conn. or Maine. From now until this
war ends I guess I'll just keep the Iris tied to the
dock. Maybe I'll take her out sometimes, just to let
her feel the wind. It's Dec. and it's cold and we
have fires and last night Lucy and Tony and Mom
and Dad and me roasted weners. Dad said let's not
listen to the 6 o'clock news tonight let's just eat
these weners and think good thots. We all did.
Later on we all admited our good thots were about
you. Hurry up and end this war Olly. I'm at the
end of the space I have to write in. Love Your
brother Alex. I sure do miss you Olly.

1

"*Let us in. Let us in, Alex.*"

Alex tried to select individual snowflakes approaching the window and follow their flight until they tapped at the glass and melted.

Each one made its plea for all the others. "*Let us in, let us in, Alex.*"

Tap, tap. Hundreds of taps. Thousands. Millions. "*Let us in, let us in.*"

The silence and warmth in this bedroom that had once been Oliver's and the attention to the gentle flow of snow made him drowsy. Outside the thin window-pane, he knew, the air was cold enough to freeze his eyelashes. The flakes of snow, usually so soft and wet, so silent, now struck the glass like tiny fragments of metal. Tap, tap, tap. They did not melt and disappear as they had earlier in the day. Frozen, solid, they were accumulated along each crosspiece in the window, forming stripes of white, puffy cotton.

Still at the window, almost hypnotized by the falling snow, Alex absently reached out to touch the edge of the Pequod High pennant tacked to the wall.

On Saturdays like this, before the war, Alex would come into the room to lie on the bed. Oliver, standing at the window, would gaze out across the field at the coast and the always heaving sea. "The very best place in the whole world, Alex."

3

How many times had Oliver said that? Fifty? A hundred?

Yes, this was the very best place in the world.

The field leading from the front porch down to the cliff had yielded to the snow, permitting itself to be covered with whiteness. But the naked granite rocks rising from the pebbled beach, as well as the dark beach itself, scorned the snow, refusing to retain even the most obstinate flakes. Of course the tides and the wind-swept mist helped, washing beach and rocks every few hours. Not even the gulls or terns dared perch for more than a minute to rest or scout food in the great sweep of the sea.

Farther up from the house, across the field toward Pequod Road, the frozen earth had accepted and held its snow since early December. Beyond the road the yards and roofs of Pequod, still holding earlier deposits that had refused to dissolve, showed yesterday's layer of white above the darker, older snow. The fishing boats at the ends of the docks, tugging at their anchors and ropes, appeared to be seeking escape from the winds and waves and snow.

Alex left the window and sat on the bed he'd inherited when Oliver went into the army. He could still hear the snowflakes tapping at the window, but he was interested in other sounds. Real sounds. The sounds of voices. He stretched the length of the bed and reached out to the domed Atwater-Kent his father had restored just for him, so he could listen to the radio at night before he fell asleep.

His sister, Lucy, hadn't approved. "I say he'll just listen to the war news and have nightmares."

"Well," his father had replied, "I say he'll have nightmares if he doesn't listen. What do you say, Alex?"

"I say I'd sure like to have the radio in my room, Dad. You can come in and listen to it, Lucy, whenever you want." Lucy's response had been a wink and a grin and a kiss, which Alex pretended to duck, blown from her hand. "I'll come in and play Glenn Miller or Tommy Dorsey," Lucy said. "If you're nice to me, I'll teach you to dance."

Alex reduced the volume so his mother and father, who were having a rare Saturday afternoon nap in their bedroom down the hall, wouldn't wake up. He caught the station knob between thumb and forefinger and rolled it gently, moving through a variety of voices. Twelve o'clock. Time for the noon news. The latest war reports.

> *Guadalcanal . . . the First Cavalry . . . General MacArthur vows . . . the Japanese Admiralty declared today . . . reports of German advances in the Ardennes. . . .*

There!

He rolled the knob back and forth for the best reception. American forces in Germany . . . the Ardennes: that was what he'd been searching for.

> *The enemy is employing considerable armor and is progressing westward. Our air force remains grounded because of the weather. . . .*

Maybe there'd be news about the 101st Airborne; maybe there'd be an interview with Oliver. That happened sometimes. A combat reporter would find a rifleman or a machine gunner from some little town and would relay the man's voice across the ocean to the plains of Kansas or Iowa or clear across the continent to California. Just last week Alex had heard an interview with a Corporal Clayton Shields from some tiny town called Occidental, California. Three weeks ago a private, a scout in the Third Division, named Walter Abercrombie, had talked about being homesick for his family in Mystic, Connecticut. He couldn't wait to get back to skiing and ice skating in the mountains and on the ponds of Connecticut. Mystic was less than ten

5

miles from Pequod. Maybe Sergeant Oliver Kellar from Pequod, Connecticut, would be interviewed soon. It could happen.

. . . In gaining this degree of surprise the enemy is favored by the weather. For some days aerial reconnaissance has been impossible, and without aerial reconnaissance it is impossible to determine the locations and movements of major reserves in the rear of the German lines.

Would Oliver, when he came home, talk about his war adventures? Would he be different? Had the war changed him? He'd been slightly wounded a month ago, receiving a Purple Heart medal, but he'd gone right back into battle. Would he still want to go fishing and hiking, would he still grab Alex and throw him on the ground and wrestle with him? Fishing and hiking and wrestling were fun. Did war make you want never to have fun again? He thought of all the war movies he'd seen. No one in those movies laughed much, no one seemed to have fun.

Would the world, Alex wondered, ever be at peace again?

Peace meant there was no war. Peace meant fun, not just dark sadness, grim despair. The movies and the radio programs and the newspapers would no longer be filled with the words *bomb* and *kill* and *death*.

Peace. No war.

Alex had to work hard to remember when the radio and the newspapers and the movies and the conversations at home as well as at Lucy's café and the classes at school were not concerned with the war.

War! *The* War!

Of course Alex wanted the war to end, but he had to admit to a touch of disappointment, perhaps even regret. With the war ending soon he himself, Alex Kellar, would not have had a chance to prove his own bravery, to prove his own loyalty to his country. He

6

would not have had a chance to kill those evil people trying to control the world.

Those evil people.

"What is the enemy called?" Miss Guthrie, the sixth-grade teacher, had asked. "The name they go by?"

Alex's was the only arm to rise.

"Alex?"

"The Nazis."

"Is that right, class?"

Howard Lynn said, "The Japs."

"Nazis and Japs. Is that the right answer? We . . . the nations we're allied with . . . *allied* with . . . we're called the Allied powers. The Allies. They, the enemy, they're called what?"

Alex: "The Axis powers. Germany and Japan and Italy."

"Correct. Good for you, Alex."

Correct, yes. But for Alex the enemy—the real, the only, enemy—was those gray-uniformed, steel-helmeted soldiers trying to kill his brother over there in Germany, those same soldiers Oliver was trying to kill. Those Nazis. Germans were called *Nazis*.

"Mom, what's it called when two things, two words, mean the same thing?"

This had been at the supper table. It would have to have been a Saturday or Sunday night because his mother and father were home for supper only on weekends. During the week they worked the night shift at the submarine base in New London, leaving home at four o'clock.

His mother had said, "They're called synonyms."

"*Germans* is a synonym for *Nazis*. Right?"

His mother and father, and his sister, Lucy, and Tony, Lucy's boyfriend, wondered about that for a while, even argued about it. Were all Germans Nazis? All Nazis Germans? Were Italian or Japanese soldiers Nazis? They didn't live in Germany. Tony said, "The Italians, they're called Fascists. But hey, I'm Italian. I

7

tried to get in the army, I wanted to fight in Italy for the good old USA. My father hates Mussolini. Calls him a crook."

The argument—well, it wasn't really an argument—went on until it was time for Lucy and Tony to leave. They were driving to New London to see *Winged Victory*, a new movie with Dana Andrews. "I'm using my last gas ration stamp for the month," Tony said, winking at Lucy. "That shows how much I love you."

Alex groaned and pretended he was about to vomit, but his mother and father beamed. Lucy pushed Tony's shoulder. "You're full of gas," she said.

Alex stood at the window. The gray cumulus clouds balanced on the eastern horizon seemed unwilling to move toward the shore, but they were not unwilling to puff themselves higher and higher, inflating their bulk with darkness.

Two o'clock. In an hour he'd have to pick up his papers and start delivering them to the houses on his route. The papers would be thinner today, Saturday, than they'd been yesterday, but the storm promised to be more severe. He probably wouldn't be able to reach the Strobles' house. Or the Blascos'. Well, no matter what the weather was like, he would be sure to get the Kilroys their paper. The radio and the newspaper were the old ladies' only links to the outside world.

Alex snapped on his high galoshes, wrapped himself in sweaters and a jacket, and tramped through knee-high snow down Pequod Road to Larry Cobb's house. It took about a minute to convince Larry that even though Christmas vacation had just begun there might be some kids from their class at the playground. They could tramp out a circle in the snow and play fox and geese. No teachers, no janitors, no little kids. Just the eighth-graders, all of them celebrating their last winter at Pequod Elementary. Larry called it Peapod.

The playground was empty. The snow stretched like clean, white cotton across the flat plane of the yard, although in the shadowed corners where the sun never reached there were drifts as high as their hips.

They clawed up the brick facings to peer through the iced windows. As they chased each other through the snow, in and out of the swings, they grabbed and rattled the chains. With lengths of fallen branches they took turns breaking icicles from every roofline they could reach. The playground's snow was no longer unblemished.

Alex led the way to the cliff above the rocky coastline. "Look at those clouds." He pointed out to sea. Lower now, as if a giant, unseen hand were pressing them from above, the clouds seemed interested suddenly in trying to reach the shore. They were tumbling forward slowly across the dark green waves.

"Storm comin'," Larry said.

"Want to help me deliver my papers? We could finish before it hits."

"I don't know," Larry said. "I'm supposed to be home early. Pap'll put the belt to me if I'm late again."

"You won't be late. The first half of the route, working together, we'll move fast. We could even pick up enough time to go on the rocks if we want to. I bet yesterday's storm brought in lots of good stuff."

Alex knew that the promise of a treasure hunt along the coast would be too much for Larry to resist. The one way he could escape his father's belt was to bring home a special bit of loot carried to shore from some unfortunate boat. "It's gonna snow for ten years," Alex said, pointing again to the east. "Look at the size of those clouds. They're moving faster. Come on, Lare. We work together we can do it."

The clouds, stuffed to their edges with blackness and not at all intimidated by the pounding surf, seemed to be racing each other westward toward the land.

Eighteen *Courier-Journal*s left, only four of them folded and ready to be tossed.

Alex eased the canvas bag from his shoulder, dropped it at his feet, and leaned forward to stretch the ache out of his back. Together, he and Larry had made more progress than he'd expected they would. Of course Larry wanted a chance at the loot that might be waiting among the rocks, but it wasn't just the loot that had convinced him to help. It was one more chance to demonstrate his gratitude for Alex's kindness. Alex was just about the only kid at school who did not tease Larry. Everyone else called him Blubber and Blimp and Lard Bucket, and worse. Alex called him Larry. Not Fat Larry but Larry. Or Lare. Limited in vocabulary and limited even more in the ability or willingness to put his feelings into words, Larry almost thanked Alex for thinking he could help.

Still bent, feeling the ache escaping, Alex considered the rocks he'd already crossed. Some were larger than houses, others larger than two houses put together.

In the east, between him and the horizon, the snow was falling faster, thicker, not swirling now but falling almost in straight vertical lines. Balanced on top of the rock, Alex tried to see inside the snow mist, tried to locate Larry among the rocks. He checked his wristwatch and sat on the stuffed canvas bag. He'd wait five minutes. If Larry didn't show up in five minutes, he'd retrace his steps and try to find him.

Alex lifted his body just enough to free one of the papers. Before the front page disappeared into the settling snow, he read aloud the banner headline at the top of the page: 9 MORE DAYS UNTIL CHRISTMAS.

The headline across the news portion: AMMUNITION SHORTAGE IN GERMAN ARMY.

He would have read the story, or part of it, if at that moment he hadn't heard Larry's call. The figure making its way across the rocks, its broad, red face streaming water, could have been a solitary sea beast washed ashore by the storm, but a mittened hand waved and a round, red mouth called, "Alex, hey Alex, wait up."

Alex shouted, "Let's go, Lare. We'll get hot chocolate at the Kilroys'."

Alex estimated that working together, and moving as fast as they had until now, they could complete the route in fifteen minutes. It was four fifteen right now, maybe four thirty. If they didn't accept the Kilroys' invitation to stop in, he could be home in time to hear the five o'clock news report on the radio. When the red hair and the freckled face appeared, Alex shouldered his canvas bag and glanced down before he leapt to the next rock, expecting to see treasure no more exciting than what they'd seen so far: a piece of lobster pot or a cork float or scraps of useless lumber. But there, tucked between two rocks, lay a load of laundry. He scrambled down, intending to hide it from Larry's view until the last minute.

The dark coat was visible first. Then a pair of dark trousers. Two black socks. A shoe. A shoe in a bag of laundry?

A shoe. A single shoe. But two socks. And a trouser leg torn along the seam, exposing a blue leg and a fragment of underwear. A blue leg. A bloated, glistening blue leg.

Alex clutched at a protruding lump of rock. The shout escaped after three tries. "Larry!"

He slid free from the canvas strap and slowly lowered himself to his stomach.

Larry arrived, panting from exertion and dripping water from galoshes and jacket. A small pool formed around his feet. His voice was almost a whisper. "Is it real, Alex?"

Alex ignored the water lapping at his galoshes. The side of the man's face that was visible looked as if a prankster had been here earlier to paint the skin dark

11

blue. The left eye pondered the left hand, fixed like a chicken's claw before his face. The right eye, the entire right side of the man's face—cheek and nose and chin—was embedded in a cushion of sand that sucked water in and thrust it out, raising the head in the process, then lowering it, then raising it.

Larry struggled down the last three or four feet of rock and stopped directly behind Alex. With both hands clinging tightly to the belt of Alex's jacket, Larry matched his moves, even stepping into his footprints. Satisfied finally that the hand would never move again, Alex leaned forward until his face hovered just inches above the black suit coat. "He's dead. We found a dead man, Lare."

"A . . . a dead man."

"He doesn't look like anyone from Pequod." Fat Larry's voice sounded as if he'd been running fast for several hours.

Alex tried to speak casually, but his voice had to fight its way out of his throat. "He's not a fisherman or a sailor."

"He's not a fisherman or a . . . how do you know that, Alex?"

"He's wearing a dark suit and a white shirt and a necktie. And dress shoes."

"One dress shoe."

Alex nudged the body with the toe of his right boot.

"Maybe he fell off a liner," Larry said. "Maybe he tried to swim ashore. He didn't make it. The tide brought him in."

"He'd be rotten by now. He'd smell bad."

"I ain't gettin' close enough to see how he smells, Alex."

"He wasn't very smart," Alex said. "Trying to swim in that sea, in a storm. Without taking off his shoes or his suit coat."

Alex knelt next to the body, gripped the edge of the coat between thumb and forefinger, and snapped the

12

coat open. He probed the inside pocket. Empty. Alex tugged at the right rear pocket of the trousers until he succeeded in withdrawing a soggy wallet.

Larry gasped. "Look at all that money."

Five twenties, three tens, three fives, four ones. "One hundred forty-nine dollars," Alex said. "He must be rich, carrying that much money on him."

Larry whistled. "One hundred and forty-nine bucks. What Pap would do with that."

Alex pulled out a driver's license. "George H. Barrows, 117 West 112th St., New York City." A Social Security card had the same name and the number 129-81-1821. And three photographs: an attractive woman with long, dark hair and a slight smile; the same woman with a ten- or twelve-year-old girl (they were holding hands, standing in what looked like a big city); and the little girl, on her knees at the side of a large Irish setter, hugging the dog.

Larry stepped back from the corpse and looked around, as if expecting someone. "We oughta get going, Alex. This is too spooky. This dead guy layin' here and those pictures. They're probably home waitin' for him. Let's go. But what about the money? We aren't gonna leave it here, are we?"

Alex dropped the retrieved wallet into his canvas paper bag. "We better go tell the police."

"Hey, let's split the money, Alex."

"What about the police? They'll know."

"They'll never know. How could they? OK, we leave ten bucks, fifteen maybe. That's what most guys would carry. A hundred and forty-nine bucks. You know how long you'd have to carry papers to make one hundred and forty-nine bucks, Alex?"

What was half of $149? $74.50. He'd have to carry papers for more than a year to make $74.50. Alex removed the wallet from his bag and held the money. It was soggy, heavy in his hand. He shoved it all into Larry's hand. "You take it. I don't want any."

13

Larry protested, insisting that Alex deserved half. He'd found the dead man, he'd even touched the guy, he'd gone into the pocket for the wallet. When Alex shook his head, seeming not to hear him, or to agree with him, Larry said, "OK," and stuffed the money in his pocket. "A hundred and forty-nine smackeroos. I'll say we found it in a can under a rock. No, in a box that washed ashore. How's that sound, Alex?"

"The police station's five miles away," Alex said.

"My house is closer than yours. If we had a phone we could go there and call the station."

"The café."

Larry agreed. "Yeah. The café. Why?"

Alex started running, the canvas bag bouncing on his hip. Lucy would be working at the café. She'd know what to do.

Lucy did know what to do. She called the police. Alex and Larry led Lucy, the two officers, and four curious customers who canceled their chowder-and-burger orders back along the asphalt road and down Perez Wharf to the rocks.

After the cops and the four men carried the sheet-wrapped body to the pickup truck that served as Pequod's ambulance, Chief Burnham asked Alex and Larry several questions. The boys responded truthfully to every question except one.

"Did you see a suitcase or wallet or anything like that?"

Alex seemed to be thinking, to be remembering. Actually, he was debating the possibility of turning over the wallet. But it would be empty. Without even a single dollar. He'd surely be suspected of taking whatever money had been there. While he was constructing the probable question-and-answer routine, Larry piped up, quite clearly and emphatically, "We didn't find anything. We just wanted to get outta there. We never saw a dead man before. Right, Alex?"

Lucy put her arm around Alex. "You did the right thing, hon. Me, I would have probably fainted right here on the rocks."

When the crowd drove off, Alex and Larry started running to finish delivering the papers. Few of the remaining customers on the route complained. The news had preceded them, so that at each house Alex and Larry were compelled to reenact their adventure.

Snow was falling heavily as they approached the Mc-Caffreys', just below the Kilroys' house. They were pushing through the snow when a girl's voice behind them called out, "Larry, wait."

Larry's sister Amelia caught up with them. "Lawrence, you better come home. Mom's mad. I bet you get a beating. They kept supper for you. I bet you go to bed without any supper at all. And wait till Pap sees your wet clothes. Boy, will you get whipped."

"Wanna bet?" Larry laughed. He raced ahead of his sister, both of them slipping and sliding in the snow. "See you, Alex. Don't find any more dead men." Alex heard him laughing. He was shouting at Amelia, "I bet he doesn't whip me. How much you wanna bet? A hundred dollars?"

The Kilroys' house was the last one on the route. Alex entered the gate, prepared to insist he didn't have time for the usual hot chocolate tonight.

He approached the stairway on the outside wall of the house leading to the upstairs entry, but Rosie Kilroy charged out and down the stairs to grab him by his shoulders and hustle him across the yard, back the way he'd come. Usually on such winter days she was wrapped in jackets and scarves and overshoes, but now she was only wearing her tattered old housecoat and bedroom slippers.

"Take your paper back. I don't want you delivering your old *Courier-Journal* here anymore. And don't de-

15

liver my food from Critchlow's. And you bring any fish I'll stuff them down your throat. I hate fish. So's my mother."

Shouting, waving whichever arm happened to be free, Rosie pushed Alex clear to the crippled gate. Then she whirled to pick her way through the jungle of frozen, stunted shrubs and fragments of masonry and lumber and rusted tools. It was hard to know if she was weeping or shouting as she climbed the stairs. At the top landing, the kitchen door opened before she reached it. It permitted her skinny body entry, then it slammed shut.

Alex kicked the gate as he passed it. She must have gone crazy. People at Joe Critchlow's store said it was just a matter of time. Maybe it had happened.

He rolled up his empty canvas bag, wondering who would now do Rosie's chores on Saturdays. Who'd deliver the groceries? He'd tell his father not to bring the Kilroys fish anymore. They brought a bit of their catch every weekend, but if she didn't want it, well, his mother would find a use for it. Why would she have said she hated fish? It wasn't true. His father and Oliver and he himself had been bringing the old women fish for as long as he could remember.

As he shifted the rolled bag in his hands, something fell to the ground. Except for one black corner, it all but disappeared in the snow. The wallet.

Alex stared at it. He'd forgotten it. Its appearance reminded him of his having committed what could be called a crime. *Could be* if he was found out.

He certainly didn't want to keep the wallet. In fact, whatever wrong he might have committed could be corrected now by giving the wallet to the police. But wait. Both he and Larry had already said there had been no wallet. By now Larry had dropped the money into his father's hands. Chief Burnham would be suspicious of an empty wallet. A man dressed in a suit carrying an empty wallet? No one would believe him.

Alex's eyes focused on an uncapped oil drum he'd passed and ignored a hundred times. Quickly, easily, naturally, he picked up the wallet and dropped it in. It remained on top of a thick puck of ice. He wrapped his hand in the canvas bag and struck the ice with the heel of his hand, but it didn't break. His cold fingers dug about in his pocket until he found his penknife. He chopped at the ice and struck it again with his fist. The ice broke, and the wallet dropped into the dark muck. Nobody would ever find it. But he'd lost his knife in the process, the knife Oliver had given him.

Alex looked back at the Kilroys' house. Upstairs, in what he knew to be a spare bedroom, the curtains were parted. A man's face hovered at the glass. It disappeared as the curtains fell back into place. But he could still see, behind the curtain, the features of the face. It wasn't Rosie or her mother. It was a man. The face moved. And disappeared.

No man had lived in that house since Rosie's father had died before Alex was born.

2

For some reasons associated with the police department's so-called ongoing investigation, the news was not made public for almost a week.

Thursday's edition of the *Courier-Journal* was special not just because its Christmas shopping insert weighed almost three pounds but because the front-page story received more column inches than the war news and included a picture of Alex Kellar and Lawrence Cobb. PEQUOD BOYS DISCOVER BODY had been set in the same type as ARDENNES BREAKTHROUGH—GERMAN ARMY ADVANCES. The map showed the black shape of the German army bulging into the white shape of Belgium.

When Alex and Larry picked up the papers for the North Pequod route, Bernard Kingsley, the owner of the newspaper, informed the boys that their photograph would be seen by fifty thousand people. He gave each of them five extra copies. "You'll want to send a copy to Oliver, Alex. He'll sure be proud of you."

Kingsley, as he spoke, glanced at the plaque above his desk. Names of the twelve *Courier-Journal* carriers who had served or were serving in the U.S. armed forces had been carved into the black walnut. Gold stars had been set in front of three of the twelve names, indicating those three men had died in the war. December 7, 1941, had been carved after the name Terrance Hanrahan.

Terry Hanrahan had been Oliver's closest friend.

He'd died in the Japanese attack on Pearl Harbor two months after he'd enlisted in the navy. His body was still inside the sunken battleship *Arizona*. Oliver, a junior in high school, had wanted to enlist immediately to avenge Terry's death, but his mother had insisted he graduate from high school first. "I have a feeling," Ethyl Kellar said, "there'll be plenty of time for revenge."

Oliver Kellar's name was eighth in the list of twelve. After hasty calculation, Alex decided that his own name would likely be located somewhere in the twenties.

Larry carried his five extra copies of the paper under his arm, refusing to permit Alex to stuff them into his canvas bag. Every so often, after tossing a folded paper onto a porch or carrying it through the snow to a front door, Larry would glance down at the front page of one of those he carried and read the caption aloud. PEQUOD BOYS DISCOVER BODY.

By the time there were only a few papers left in the bag, Larry was tired of carrying his personal copies. "OK, you can carry these. But don't fold them."

Alex pulled the bag open for Larry to place the papers in himself. The two boys in the photograph peered up at him. His own face seemed full of excitement, as if he were being acclaimed a war hero. He wasn't a hero. He'd lied. He was certain to be caught someday. All criminals were caught. He recalled the Old Wrangler's little speech at the end of all of the "Tom Mix" radio stories he'd listened to when he was five and six years old. "Straight shooters always win. Lawbreakers always lose. It pays to shoot straight." Sometimes, at supper, when Alex or Lucy would interrupt the flow of food around the table, Oliver would lower his voice and shape his thumb and forefinger into a pistol. He'd point a finger at one of the culprits. "Hey, straight shooters always win. Lawbreakers always lose. It pays to pass the beans."

"Larry, do you still have that money?" Alex asked, wishing he hadn't posed for that picture.

Larry broke into a skip and hop. "I gave Pap all but five bucks. He almost swallowed his chewin' tobacco, but he didn't even ask me where I got it. He said, 'It's about time you bring some money home.' He thinks I sold a lot of copper and brass to the junk man. Now he'll see the picture. I'm famous. Not lousy famous, like one of those gangsters on the FBI's Most Wanted list. Important famous. Good famous. That makes him famous, too. That's a good picture of me, ain't it? Except it shows you a lot taller than me. I'm laughin'. You ain't even smilin'. I ought to have kept ten bucks, not just five. Pap would never knew the difference. Hey, I could have kept fifty. He still wouldn't used the belt."

Neither Larry nor anyone else in the Cobb family could ever hope to earn much respect. The Kellars were the only people in Pequod who invited Larry inside their house. He often had supper with them. In school the other kids said he smelled bad, like he never bathed. And his grades were so bad he never earned a single silver star in front of his name on the honor roll.

It was almost impossible for Larry or his five sisters to free themselves from a crime committed by Erasmus Cobb almost two hundred years before. Erasmus, with a reputation as the village drunk, had betrayed thirty young American rebels to the British army. All had been executed. The reward: a small keg of brandy, which was consumed in a space of six hours, and a lead ball in the back of the head ten minutes after the young rebels had been executed. "It's in the blood" was the comment that ran from house to house, from year to year.

Unable to fight free from a condemnation born before he was, Larry's father had decided to live by his wits. As a result he'd twice been convicted of raiding his neighbors' lobster pots, a crime comparable to cattle rustling out west, often with the same gory consequences. In spite of the contempt they endured, the entire Cobb family continued to appear together in church every Sunday morning.

"Alex?"

"What?"

"Would you read some of the story?"

"What story?"

"In the paper. I can't read that small print. My eyes. I need glasses. Use one of your own papers though. OK?"

Alex huddled over the paper, shifting to catch whatever light he might find. As he read, he had to keep shaking the snow off the paper.

Two boys discovered the body of a man yesterday on a stretch of isolated beach a half mile north of Pequod. Alex Kellar and Lawrence Cobb, of Pequod, while delivering the *Courier-Journal*, wandered down to the beach to search for wreckage deposited by the storm. The body, apparently washed up by the waves, was trapped between two rocks.

The victim, 30 to 35 years of age, has blond hair and blue eyes. He is six feet tall and weighs 185 pounds. He apparently drowned. There is no evidence of trauma. The body contains no significant scars. His tweed suit contains a Hart Schaffner & Marx label. Details will be forthcoming as the investigation continues.

Preliminary examination of the clothing indicates the trousers, without cuffs, had 5 or 6 years of wear. For this reason investigators estimate the suit to have been purchased just before the war. Cuffless trousers were first offered in 1940 to save fabric for army and navy uniforms so this substantiates the assumed dating.

"What's *traw-ma* mean, Alex? There was no evidence of *traw-ma*. You think that means taking a wallet?"

Alex brushed the snow from the thoroughly damp front page. After folding the paper carefully, he returned it to the canvas bag, which now contained four papers for subscribers and the ten extra supplied by Bernard Kingsley.

The wallet.

The best thing to do, he decided, was to ask Larry to return the money so they could . . . could what? So they could recover the wallet from the old drum near the Kilroys' house? So they could then replace the money? And then hand everything over to the cops?

Alex watched Larry open the Huntsingers' gate and walk up the path of packed snow to the porch. Larry waited for Mrs. Huntsinger to appear, Alex knew, to congratulate him, actually to notice his existence for the first time, but Mrs. Huntsinger was not at home. The Huntsingers had a son in the army and one in the navy, and, like his own parents, they gave every spare minute to volunteer service at the USO in New London. They baked cookies and wrote letters for servicemen and were always available for the lonely young men who missed the affection of older people. Alex's father and Peter Huntsinger worked as a team two nights a week when they served as air wardens. They met at one or the other's home whenever possible to play (cards that had silhouettes of German airplanes on their backs.) Their conversation was a mix of poker and air raid practice. "I'll take two . . . that's a Fokker . . . full house . . . Stuka 122 . . . queens for openers . . . that's a Messerchmitt . . . that's a Junkers . . ."

"I'm hungry," Larry said. "Hey, maybe the Loony Ladies will give us hot chocolate and cookies."

Alex hurried on. "The McCaffreys are the last customer now." He stopped and looked back, as much at the Kilroys' house behind Larry as at Larry himself. "The Kilroys canceled."

"You took them one the other night. You were going there when I ran home with Amelia."

"Rosie told me. She said she didn't want me coming around anymore." Alex almost broke his vow to hoard the mystery of that face at the window. But if he told it to Larry, it would be broadcast to every kid in Pequod before Christmas. Every night kids would be hiding in the bushes surrounding the Kilroy house, hoping to collect their own spook stories.

That face had no special meaning anyhow. It could only have been Old Clara.

Friday nights were Alex's favorite, because he came to the Pequod Café, where Lucy worked, for supper. He paid his way, Tony reminded him, because he often helped clear tables and did odd jobs in the kitchen, peeling potatoes or cleaning crabs or washing dishes. Alex did not consider it work. He got to listen to the latest stories about the war, feeling very much a part of the home front, where, President Roosevelt often reminded the nation, the war could be won or lost. With their victory gardens and their collections of fat, paper, cloth, metal, string, with their volunteer warden patrols, their acceptance of the rationing of gas and butter and coffee—they were as heroic as those men on the front lines.

Tonight, as most nights, few kids were in the café. But the adults there—fishermen and their wives, defense plant workers, soldiers and sailors and pilots home on leave or escaping from the various army or navy bases for a few unregimented hours, girlfriends catching momentary joy in the safety of their mates— they all talked of the war, debating the information about the latest land or sea battles. Even the fishermen talked not of boats or weather or catches but of who'd been drafted, who'd enlisted, who'd been wounded, who'd been killed. Five women from Pequod had joined the armed forces. Tonight two of them, one in the brown uniform of the WACs and one in the blue uniform of the WAVES, were respected as much as the men were. The WAC, a lieutenant, knew as much about the air force as any male pilot. She'd been flying C-47s and other planes to London for a year. A plane she'd been piloting had even been attacked by a German Messerschmitt, and one of the ribbons on her jacket was the Purple Heart.

The café was pretty upbeat tonight. The news about the German breakthrough was not given too much attention. We'd won too many battles already, the Germans had lost too many men, too much land. Victory was inevitable. This was Hitler's last gasp.

The paper Santa Claus and reindeer taped to the wall behind the counter, the Christmas tree on top of the counter, next to the cash register, the sprigs of mistletoe hanging from strategic doorways all contributed to a promise of new joy.

Tony had to hire two extra waitresses and a dishwasher on Friday nights. His mother helped in the kitchen. Tony had lost a leg in a fishing run when he was sixteen, but he defied anyone to better him on a boat, on a field, or on a dance floor. He'd tried to get into the service four times, but each time, when he'd received his physical, he'd been turned away. "One doctor just up and laughed when he saw me standing there naked, balancing myself on my one leg. You know something? On that one good leg, I could have taken on any man in the hall."

Lucy, speeding out of the kitchen with several plates balanced on her outstretched left arm, shouted, "Hey, gang, here he is. Our hero!" Several customers, who'd known Alex all his life, cheered. Alex felt his face turn hot and red, and he lowered his head. Lucy and everyone else, thinking him too humble, patted his back and praised him, and one of the few kids around came to him to ask what the dead man looked like. Alex shrugged him off.

The front page of the *Courier-Journal* was tacked to

the wall of the passageway near the cash register. An elderly couple, probably tourists, hovered there, reading the story, glancing occasionally at Alex.

As soon as she was free, Lucy scooped Alex into her arms. "Hi, honey. You get a call from Hollywood yet?" She held him at arm's length and asked the entire café and everyone as far away as Boston, "Isn't my kid brother a handsome hero? He looks like Cary Grant and Gary Cooper and Clark Gable mixed into one."

Alex ducked under her arms and escaped into the kitchen, where Tony and Mrs. Alda were cooking. "Hey, Champ," Tony called. "How's it feel having your mug pasted all over the front page? How many autographs you have to sign? Betty Grable and Rita Hayworth called. They asked if you're free tonight. They want you in their next movie. You got it made, kid."

"Come on, Tony. It wasn't anything. The guy was dead. We just found him. Anyone could have done that. I'd really have been a hero if I'd found him before he died. And saved him."

"Yeah," Lucy said, arranging a new selection of steaming plates along her left arm, "but then it wouldn't be a mystery. Right? We'd know who he is. This way, well, anything could happen. Maybe he's rich. Maybe he's a prince. His family could offer you a Rolls-Royce and a castle in France."

Tony waved a spatula in the air and laughed. "Yeah, the Rolls-Royce sits there 'cause there's no gas and the castle's a wreck 'cause it's been bombed by the Nasties."

"No imagination," Lucy replied, winking at Alex. "Watch the third stool, honey. Erik Winkleman's on his last cup of coffee. I hope."

When Erik Winkleman pushed his truck-sized body from the counter, Alex sat on the vacated stool and pretended to be bored with the continuing attention from the neighboring stools.

"How you doin', honey?" Lucy asked, as she wiped

the counter before him and offered him the setup of napkin, utensils, water glass, coffee cup. As she poured the ice water into the glass she whispered, "I got the radio on in the kitchen. In case there's news. Tony told me some general was just interviewed by Lowell Thomas. Said the German army was so low on ammunition it can't keep fighting more than a week, maybe two. Do you believe it? Oliver might be home soon. We'll have the biggest party Pequod's ever seen. What would you like, honey?" She pretended to resettle his napkin so her mouth could be close to his ear. "We got some special beef from a farm in Rhode Island. Want the beef?"

"How about the beef and a bowl of chowder?" Alex watched a large slice of lemon custard pie being set before the man on his right and knew what he'd have for dessert. His mouth was savoring the future tartness when a hand fell on his shoulder. He turned, expecting it to be some new admirer, but found Chief Burnham grinning at him. He could barely swallow the lump in his throat. He'd admit to having found the wallet. He'd offer to go get it immediately. He'd face whatever embarrassment followed and accept his punishment.

"Hey," the chief said. "Am I that ugly? You went white as that napkin."

"You surprised me." Alex tried to laugh off his fright. "I thought you were someone else."

"Who? King Kong? I just wanted to thank you again, Alex. You're gonna send that story to Oliver, ain't you? Tell him I said hello, tell him the town's prayin' for him." He squeezed Alex's shoulder. "He'll be OK, kid."

Fortunately a few other customers required the chief's attention, firing questions faster than he could respond. Had he found out who the man was? Had the man died or been killed? Where was he from? Chief Burnham assured them that at the moment they knew as much as he did. Maybe . . . in a day or two . . .

26

Alex forced his attention to stay on the food even as he listened to the chief. He glanced up finally and, in silence, read the posters on the wall. He knew every word, every illustration, but for now they could distract him from thoughts about that wallet.

The posters, on every wall of the café, advised all that A SLIP OF THE LIP CAN SINK A SHIP, and, to assure eventual victory, BUY U.S. BONDS, and WASTE NOT—WANT NOT.

On the jukebox the Andrews Sisters were singing "Don't sit under the apple tree with anyone else but me." Lucy, as she swept by, sang along and pinched Alex. "No, no, no, don't sit under the apple tree with anyone else but me, anyone else but me, anyone else but me, till I come marching home."

The last bite of the lemon pie just would not go beyond the back of his mouth, when, glancing into the mirror, Alex noticed Chief Burnham. The chief was listening to one of the many people gathered around him, but he was watching Alex. Or was that his imagination? He almost brought up his entire meal. But if he didn't look pleased, Lucy would think he was sick. It had to have been his imagination, because the chief, leaving with the last customers, smiled at Alex and waved two fingers in a V-for-victory sign.

Alex helped the dishwasher and the extra waitresses scrub the floors of the dining room and the kitchen. Tony and his mother put the kitchen in order, and Lucy arranged the tables for the next day's breakfast. Whenever she happened to be near the jukebox, she slipped in two or three nickels. When now and then she grabbed Alex and carried him across the floor as if he was her dancing partner, he could not deny the sweet, crazy buzz in his head.

Lucy accompanied every vocalist, meshing her voice with Sinatra (*Embrace me, my sweet embraceable you . . .*) with Helen O'Connel (*Tangerine, you are all they claim . . .*) and with the ever-present Andrews Sisters (*. . . he's in the army now, he's blowin' reveille, he's the boogie-woogie bugle boy from Company B. . .*).

Tony came out of the kitchen, grabbed Lucy, and, both of them sharing the lyrics, he tossed Lucy into the air and down and under his legs. He pivoted on his good leg to catch her hands and bring her up on the beat. "Get them generals in here," Tony shouted. "If I can jitterbug, I can be a soldier." At which point he lost his balance and the two of them collapsed, laughing, onto the floor.

Alex usually walked Lucy home around eleven o'clock. If Tony had successfully bartered with one of his customers for an extra gas-ration stamp he'd drive them home in his '37 Chevy. He drove them tonight, the Chevy's bald tires slipping and sliding on the snow. "Three are smooth as a baby's bottom," he said. The moderately grooved right front tire had been traded recently for fifteen free suppers.

At home, in the semidarkness, with Tony and Lucy murmuring in the kitchen, Alex listened to Lucy's records on Oliver's old phonograph, which Tony had miraculously rehabilitated. He closed his eyes and sang some of the lyrics to himself, trying to imagine himself moving along a dance floor like Fred Astaire. Then he was vaguely aware of being clutched in Tony's arms, being lifted, being half-walked, half-carried, up the stairs to his bedroom.

Before he dropped into deep sleep, he heard his mother and father stomping their feet on the front porch, heard their voices in the entryway, on the stairs. The blankets were drawn up to his chin, the radio was turned on, a voice murmured something that might be words. He tried to find the strength to force himself fully awake so he might confess everything. But then a wallet, *the* wallet, bloomed and circled the room like an orbiting moon. In the light from the moon-wallet, his mother and father, in their soiled work clothes, reached for the black leather that remained beyond their fingers. Chief Burnham was sitting in the town's pickup, scowling through the window on the driver's side. He pulled himself out of the seat and joined not just Alex's mother and father but Oliver, who must have been there, unseen, the entire time. The chief glanced at Alex, shook his head in grave concern, then leaned over to whisper in Oliver's ear. The wallet, now a black, hairy bat, wheeled about to attack him, slapping at his face with its brittle leather wings.

Alex tried to throw up his hands to hold the fanged bat at bay, but his arms refused to move. "Momma, Poppa," Alex cried, "help me."

The radio voice went silent. A large, warm hand—human, real—caressed his forehead. "It's OK, it's OK, son." His father's voice, as warm as his hand, led Alex back into sleep.

3

Saturday morning.

Alex sat at Oliver's desk in Oliver's bedroom. Behind him the closet was still half-filled with Oliver's clothes.

Dear Oliver was all he'd written so far, and he'd been sitting here for at least fifteen minutes. He raised his eyes to the photographs on the wall above the desk.

There was Oliver on his first day of basic training.

Dear Alex, I just got my GI haircut. I have ears. I never saw them before. Olly.

In new, creased suntans, tie tucked inside the shirt at the third button, cotton overseas cap tilted down toward his right eye.

Dear Alex, Finishing basic training next week. Thinking about joining the paratroopers. You can't tell in the black and white picture but the braid on my cap is blue. Blue braid shows I'm in the Infantry. Olly.

In combat fatigues, a steel helmet low over the eyes and strap tight under the chin, jump boots tightly laced, a revolver in a holster on his hip, a knife tucked into the top of the right boot, a bulky parachute pack on his back, harness straps across his chest.

Dear Alex, Final jumps today. Three of them. I get
my paratroop wings tomorrow. I'll be going into
the Hundred First Airborne, the Screaming Eagle
Division. Olly.

In camouflage fatigues, standing with three other
men, all of them sunburned, all of them young and
defiant.

Dear Alex, 2 men in my squad. My buddies. God
have mercy on them Germans because we sure
won't. Cpl. Oliver Kellar.

On the upper left arm of each man: the head of a
screaming eagle. Under the eagle head on Oliver's arm:
two chevrons.

The last letter from Oliver had come from "Somewhere in Europe." For six months Oliver had defied all
odds. In a story in *Life* magazine an infantry captain,
interviewed by the writer, said that squad leaders disappear faster than candy bars. "In combat," the captain said, "if a squad leader lasts three months, he
better quit. He's beat the odds. From then on every
hour, every minute, could be his last."

If the war was to end soon, *if* those reports of the
German army's shortage of ammunition were true, *if*
Oliver's luck should hold, *if* maybe he had a wound just
serious enough to take him out of combat. *If . . . if . . .
if . . .*

Will Oliver get to read this letter? He won't if it's
not written. If you write it, Alex, you could be contrib-
uting to that collection of *if* miracles that might keep
him alive. If you *don't* write it now, you might jinx him.

Dear Oliver,
    You can see I'm not sending a V letter this
time. That's because we're not allowed to put
things in a V letter and I've got something I'm
sending you cut out of the *Courier-Journal.* People

31

are calling me and Larry heroes but we really
didn't do anything. We were running the rocks
like you used to do looking for treasure and we
found . . .

Once he'd begun, Alex could not stop writing until
he realized suddenly he was shivering. He'd have to go
down to the cellar to add coal to the furnace. There was
a better choice. He went to the closet, selected one of
Oliver's sweaters, and returned to the desk. As he took
up the writing again, he could almost smell Oliver. The
heavy sweater and the photographs kept distracting
him, but he went on, adding line after line. When he
sealed the envelope, he was quite satisfied. He'd told
the story even better than the *Courier-Journal* article
he'd included. But he'd said nothing about the wallet
or the money. And that was why he'd awakened so
early: to tell it all to Oliver, who would write back and
tell him, *"Forget it, Alex. It wasn't a crime. No one will
care. Think about important things. Like your letters to
me."*

Did you know Lucy and Tony are getting married?
In June. It would be great if the war's over and
you're home and can go to the wedding. Tony talks
a lot about being 4F. He tried to get in the service
but they kept sayin' no. He asked if the army had
suicide squads, like the Japanese. If they did he'd
volunteer for one. The army guy said the army
doesn't have suicide squads but even if they did
how could Tony charge a machine gun nest without a right leg? Tony challenged the guy to a hun-
dred-yard dash but the guy said he was only kid-
ding. One thing about having Tony in the family
though is he owns a boat twice as big and four
times as powerful as the Iris. Tony's brothers use
the boat for fishing but once Tony's in the family
you and me and Tony can go out together. Tony's
boat can probably take us to Newfoundland in a
strong blow and never even lean over. He said that
and I said I bet you.

Alex closed his eyes and saw on the inner walls of his eyelids the *Esmeralda* with the three of them working the lines, the three of them gaffing fish and swinging them over the rails and down into the ice hold. He saw the *Esmeralda* deep in the water, easing up to the dock. The *Iris* would be jealous, so he'd spend some time with her, cleaning and painting and taking her out alone once every week or two. Even with the *Esmeralda* in the family, they'd never get rid of the *Iris*.

Alex didn't hear the telephone until the third ring. He rushed downstairs to answer. Lucy lived for her Saturday mornings, when she could sleep until ten o'clock. His parents, too, slept in late on the weekends. If the phone had awakened Lucy, he'd catch it all through breakfast. But he heard no floorboards squeaking upstairs, no water running in the bathroom.

Certain that it could only be Larry calling about the afternoon movie, Alex pitched his voice high, to trick Larry into thinking he was talking to Lucy. "Sorry, Larry, Alex joined the army this morning. He's already in Germany."

"Alex, this is Rose Kilroy.

"I apologize for the way I acted, Alex. I've been sick. Momma's sick, too. We want you to keep delivering the paper."

"Sure, Rosie. I'll start after Christmas. Do you want me to do any work today or tomorrow? I didn't finish stacking the firewood last Saturday. And I'll bring your groceries from Critchlow's store, like I always . . ."

"No, no. Joe Critchlow will deliver them. They're too heavy for you."

"Rosie, I've been delivering groceries for Joe Critchlow for a year."

"Well, you have all those other people; you won't miss us. We'll pay you the twenty-five cents anyway. You better not come in the house for a while anyway. Whatever we got might be contagious. Just throw the paper on the porch. No, better yet, leave it on the

33

bottom step. We owe you for the month, so we'll pay you everything tomorrow."

"Tomorrow's Sunday. You mean Monday."

"No, I mean tomorrow. Would you go to Critchlow's tomorrow and buy me a copy of the *New York Times* and the *Boston Globe*. If you can pay for them I'll pay you back, and then I'll pay for last month's *Courier-Journal*. But can you come exactly at four o'clock, Alex?"

"What about the coal? You said it was being delivered this week. Do you want me to shovel it in the cellar?"

"No, no. Hawkins did that when he delivered it. So tomorrow at four. But remember: don't come in."

Alex returned the earpiece to its cradle and waited. Had Rosie finished talking? Something had been left unsaid. Her voice. She'd rushed through the conversation, and one thing Rosie never did was to talk fast. Well, she said she'd been sick. Tomorrow she might be better.

Tomorrow. He'd probably accompany his father tomorrow, helping collect the contributions. He'd try to convince his father to take out the *Iris* tomorrow. They'd gone out in foul weather before, and there had been some anxious moments, but it wasn't the weather, he knew, that controlled his father's needs and pleasures these days. It was this war. Well, now that the end of the war was approaching, they might be out on the water again on Saturday mornings. The three of them: his father, Oliver, and himself. And Tony, too. There'd be four now.

Alex went into the living room to wait for the ten o'clock news report.

Harry Kellar had covered a large portion of one living-room wall with a map of Europe. Blue ribbons represented the Allied lines and black ribbons the German and Italian lines. Relying on radio reports and magazines and the newspapers that came into the house, he was able to keep the positions of the two lines fairly current. Colored pins with tiny flags of red paper indicated the positions of the 101st Airborne Division, so far as they could be known.

Alex's father had been an artilleryman in the First World War, in 1918. He loved to play the historian and strategist now, proving, he maintained, that by having kept him an enlisted man, the army had lost the talents of an exceptional military tactician. During the night, after his return from warden patrol and before he went to work in New London, he worked on the colored ribbons, bringing them up to date.

There was the American First Army in Belgium, a blue ribbon curved across Germany's Siegfried Line, facing into the black area called Germany. There was the American Third Army, a blue ribbon in France, curved across the French Moselle River and not far from the German Saar River. It too was facing into the black area of Germany. The VIII Corps, including Americans and Europeans, was a blue line stretching a long distance along the Belgian and German borders.

A pin, stuck into the city of Reims, indicated the specific location of the 101st Airborne Division. Of Oliver.

After the news Alex pulled on his galoshes and jacket and walked through the snow to Larry's house. A small army of kids was playing fox and geese in the nearby field. Larry insisted he and Alex lead the kids to the rocks where they had made their now famous discovery. Near the rocks, while they were chasing each other, Larry stopped to tug at what promised to be an inner tube. Alex took hold, thinking it could be added to their collection of rubber at home.

Out of the sand came not an inner tube but a small rubber dinghy containing twenty or thirty slashes. Alex ran again, the kids behind him. Again to the café, to

Lucy, who, again, called the police. The group that descended on the site included not just Chief Burnham, local police, and several members of the Highway Patrol, but three intense, middle-aged men in dark suits and overcoats. The three local policemen held the kids at bay while the men in dark suits searched every rock and every inch of sand.

The kids gaped, gasped, whispered. "The FBI . . . that's the FBI . . . the G-men . . ."

A commentator on the evening news—the national, not local news—was the first to mention the word *saboteurs*.

Alex had won permission to bring Larry to the café for supper. Lucy, bringing them bowls of soup, stopped in front of the radio that sat on the shelf just above the chopping block. Then she set down the bowls and clanked a knife against an empty water glass. "Listen," she called, "listen."

In a report released just one hour ago, the office of the Federal Bureau of Investigation announced that slashes found on a rubber dinghy discovered on a beach near Pequod, Connecticut, had been made by a very sharp blade. Someone, the bureau went on, had tried to bury, to conceal, the rubber dinghy. That small rubber boat could possibly be related to a search the bureau is conducting for Nazi saboteurs.

There was talk of little else for the next hour, of course. Saboteurs on the Connecticut coast? Why not? New London was one of the largest submarine bases in the world, wasn't it? Could there be saboteurs in Pequod? Could someone in Pequod have Nazi sympathies? Casual glances about the room identified no suspicious strangers. Could there be Nazi lovers among old friends, lifelong neighbors?

"What's a saboteur?" Larry whispered.

"A spy."

"That boat we found. That's the one they're talking about?"

"That's the one. Yeah."

Nothing, not even the possibility of traitors or spies, could distract Larry from his food. But he did pause finally, a fork mounded with food partway to his mouth. "That guy." He let the fork and food return to his plate. "The guy we found. He could be one of them. Right?"

"I was just thinking of that. If he was a saboteur, where'd he come from? Remember that Social Security card? He had an address in New York."

No one left the café. There would be another news report at seven o'clock. New arrivals, studied as they came through the doors, shivering and shaking the snow from their boots and coats, found seats at already crowded tables. In minutes they too, informed, pondered the possibilities of enemy agents in this very room or roaming the stony hills or concealed in abandoned seashore shacks.

Lucy turned the volume of the radio high at seven o'clock.

. . . there is reason to believe that within the last week German submarines sent several saboteurs into the area of New London, Connecticut. A study of new evidence now strongly suggests that the body found by two boys on a shore near Pequod, Connecticut, was one of those saboteurs. A spokesman for the Federal Bureau of Investigation in Washington praised those boys of Pequod, especially Lawrence Cobb and Alex Kellar, who, in the space of two days, have helped the United States in its war effort every bit as much as our brave men now fighting the enemy in Europe and the Pacific.

In Belgium, where the German attack has gained the popular name of the Battle of the Bulge, General Eisenhower assures reporters that though the German armies have advanced approximately fifty miles there is no cause for panic.

At the mention of the names of the two local heroes, everyone in the room had cheered, and Lucy had left her customers to run over and throw her arms around Alex and then Larry. Tony insisted they take a second serving of his mother's chocolate cake.

The discussions returned to the possible presence of saboteurs in the hills of Pequod and how search committees ought to be organized. Various people made suggestions and even began making lists of names and what days and hours specific people might be prepared to volunteer. Then Lucy, who had returned to the radio, called out again for attention.

This is Peter Higabotham in London. General Dwight Eisenhower, supreme commander of the Allied forces in Europe, has reacted to the recent shocking victories of the German forces in Belgium. The commander, concerned about the morale of our troops, has just issued his first order of the day. It reads as follows. "By rushing out from his fixed defenses the enemy may give us the chance to turn his great gamble into his worst defeat. So I call upon every man, all of the Allies, to rise now to new heights of courage, of resolution and of effort. Let everyone hold before him a single thought—to destroy the enemy on the ground, in the air, everywhere—destroy him! United in this determination and with the unshakable faith in the cause for which we fight, we will, with God's help, go forward to our greatest victory." This is Peter Higabotham in London.

The café had grown silent. There was a grim, almost stunned, sense of possible loss in the air. As if everyone in the café was aware for the first time that Allied forces in Europe were about to be destroyed, as if this nation, which had never been defeated, was about to lose this most important war. The voice of General Eisenhower, with its attempts to stiffen the spine, had, with the suggestion that victory might not be easy, softened it. The saboteurs were forgotten. The news about the German breakthrough had been ignored. It wasn't important. General Patton would stop it in a couple of hours. But hours had passed, many hours, and those defeated Germans were continuing to advance. For General Eisenhower to say what he'd said meant the Germans were turning the tide of the war. Had already turned it. How many boys from Pequod were in the path of those German tanks and soldiers?

Lucy tried to help lift the gloom by dragging a reluctant Tony under a sprig of mistletoe and kissing him. Someone managed to find the drive to drop some coins in the jukebox. The bouncy, irreverent Andrews Sisters seemed to one woman to be in bad taste. She pulled the plug.

Lucy, irritated, plugged the jukebox back in and promised everyone all the dessert they wanted. On the house.

Alex said he'd return as soon as he walked Larry home.

On the sidewalk in front of the café, both boys pulled their stocking caps down over their ears and buttoned their jacket collars. The air was cold inside Alex's nostrils and, when he took a deep breath, at the back of his throat. Larry complained that they had no radio at home but admitted that even if they had one no one would listen to it. Larry giggled and waved his arms and shouted. "I can't believe it," he said. "You know my pap hasn't laid a hand on me since we found that guy the FBI thinks is a spy. And you know what?"

"What?"

"Two people came up to my mom at a store and asked her if she wanted a job cleaning their houses. They wouldn't have gone near Mom before. And get this. My sister Martha has actually been invited to a

New Year's Eve party. We're gonna have a swell Christmas. Real gifts for the first time. All because of you, Alex. You not taking any of the money. I'll never forget that, Alex. You're the best friend I ever had."

The snow crunched under their galoshes. Alex stopped. "It's wrong, Larry."

"What's wrong?"

"Oliver's over in Germany, fighting for our country. I took that spy's wallet and hid it. That could help the Germans. Oliver's fighting them, I'm helping them."

"*We* took that wallet, Alex. You and me both. Not just you."

"I hid it and then lied."

"*We* lied. Don't just put the blame on yourself. But what'll we do? I gave Pap the money. He won't give it back. I think he's spent it already anyway. On Christmas gifts. And Christmas supper. We're gonna have a turkey. Pap called me Santa Claus. I have four dollars left. You want that?"

"I'm going to give the wallet to the police."

"Do you have it?"

"I know where it is," Alex said.

"OK, what'll we tell them? About suddenly having a wallet when we said there wasn't any?"

"I don't know. Yeah, I do know. I'll say we went to the rocks again, looking for treasure, and we found it. They can't prove it's not true."

"Well, where'd we find it? We both have to say the same thing." Larry's persistent effort to share the responsibility surprised Alex, and pleased him. He was feeling better already.

Alex said, "We found it in the sand, under some rocks, far up the beach. And you don't even have to know where. I'll say I found it."

"But what about it being empty? He'd have a little bit, wouldn't he? Here, I'll give you my four dollars."

"No, keep it. You ought to have some money. I owe it to you anyway. You've helped a lot with my paper

40

route. I have money saved. I'll put ten or eleven dollars in it."

Larry stood there, his jacket open, as if the freezing winds were somehow missing his body. "No, that's just not right. I'll find out how much Pap's got left. I'll sneak whatever's left out of his pants. He'll be drunk. He won't remember. I'll get the money."

It was late but Alex could not go home. He was drawn back to the path of his paper route. A strange irresistible, almost tangible force caught him, pulled him, up the hill past the McCaffreys' house to the Kilroys' house.

His nose and forehead, unprotected, were so cold they burned. He had to get back to the warm café very soon. Moving slowly, hunched over, he reached the gate. The house hovered on the opposite side of the yard, in a jungle of boards and pipe and wire fencing, its dark shape outlined in a thick layer of whiteness. The pile of coal near the cellar door was completely covered with snow.

But Rosie said the coal had been hauled inside. Why would she say that? He watched the house for a moment, as if the old building would tell him. Every window was filled with light that was muted by blinds. Rosie and Old Clara were not taking chances with whatever sickness they had.

At the iron drum, about to reach down inside, Alex heard an unfamiliar call. A chill shot up his spine, through his hair. But then the sound, continuing, charmed him, held him. Was it the radio? Was someone singing? It was a violin. Someone inside was playing Rosie's old fiddle, as she called it, whenever Alex or Oliver noticed it. Covered with dust, the instrument hung from a nail on the dining-room wall. Old people in Pequod told stories about Rosie's father taking the fiddle to sea with him and how when there was a lull, day or night, his music could be heard on the breeze,

41

sounding like whales crying. Rosie had never told anyone in Pequod that she could play, and play so beauti-
fully.

Breaking free from the haunting melody, Alex removed his right glove. His fingernails could not make a
scratch on the ice.

He couldn't risk the effort to search for a stick or a
rock now. Tomorrow, when he delivered the papers,
he'd bring a hammer. He'd waited this long, one more
day wouldn't matter.

Alex was stretched out on his bed, feeling clean, not
just because he'd showered but because he'd made his
decision. That old leather wallet could have all sorts of
clues that would help the FBI. His mother and father,
having finished their shift, would be returning home
any minute. Lucy was somewhere with Tony, probably
at the café. Alex was so content he was almost asleep.
Then he sat up. The radio. A special report interrupted
the music.

> The German army has launched its massive attack on a
> sixty-mile front. From the Hürtgen Forest to the eastern
> bulge of Luxembourg, crack German armored and infantry
> divisions are driving forward. After a spell of foul weather
> has grounded Allied reconnaissance and attack planes, the
> German Luftwaffe, considered destroyed, has hurled hun-
> dreds of bombers and fighters into the support of the ground
> attack. German paratroops have landed behind the U.S. lines,
> snarling communications, and buzz bombs, new so-called
> victory weapons, are flying over the lines and into advance
> as well as rear echelons of American troops. Similar rockets
> and bombs, those buzz bombs, are now exploding on En-
> gland as well, in the already devastated city of London.
> Surprised American troops are fighting back. The crack One
> Hundred First Airborne Division as well as other American
> forces are being rushed into action. This is Eric . . .

42

Alex heard his parents stomping their feet on the front porch. When his mother entered, followed by his father, Alex said, "The Hundred First is being rushed into action in that Battle of the Bulge."

4

Alex awoke earlier than usual Sunday, but stayed in bed, inside his warm blanket-cocoon. He could not bear hearing the latest reports of continuing advances by German forces in Belgium, at the Bulge.

A few minutes before he'd heard the toilet flush and the water running in the pipes and the stairway squeaking, so he knew his father had gone downstairs to the radio in the living room. Minutes later the aroma of strong morning coffee climbed the stairs.

Once awake, Alex continued to resist the tug of the ornate Atwater-Kent at the side of his bed. He kept both arms beneath the blankets, both hands clenched at his thighs. But he could not bear the thought of missing the good news, should there be good news. As he suspected it would, his resistance thinned, then snapped. He turned the radio on.

Nothing of importance. No matter which station he tried. Everyone was being very cautious.

"You awake, Alex?"

"Morning, Dad. I'm awake. Have you heard anything?"

"The same things you've been hearing. 'Details withheld . . . serious problems . . .' All that stuff. How about running over to Critchlow's store and buying a few newspapers?" His father held two one-dollar bills in the air, then deposited them on the top of Alex's dresser.

Alex fitted a new set of long underwear over his legs and arms and added his usual complement of heavy wool socks, sweater, lumberjack shirt, navy pea coat, galoshes. After burrowing through the snow to Critchlow's store, he bought copies of all the available newspapers, including the *Times* and the *Globe*. The papers, having gone to press before the reports of the German assault had been made public, offered no news. Nowhere on the front pages was there even one word about the 101st Airborne Division.

Halfway home Alex remembered Rosie Kilroy's request, so he had to return to the store to buy extra copies of both the *Times* and the *Globe*.

Why, he wondered, would Rosie and Old Clara Kilroy suddenly be interested in the *New York Times* and the *Boston Globe*?

The day Oliver had turned over his paper route to Alex, he'd wanted to bet a dime that neither of the women ever read the *Courier-Journal*. "They save it for making fires," Oliver said, clucking his tongue. "And that radio. I bet they've forgotten they even have it. What was the last thing they heard on it? The discovery of America? 'Hey, Isabella, this is Christopher Columbus direct from the New World. I found a country here got some funny red-skinned people smoke leaves they call tobacco. Can you hear me, Isabella, my queen, over there in Spain?' "

The Kilroys' radio had to have been the first model offered by the Sears, Roebuck catalog. It needed repairs so often it was rarely used. Harry Kellar, who had a reputation for being an exceptional handyman ("Jack of all trades," he said, "master of none"), had replaced just about every tube and coil and wire. He never accepted Rosie's or Old Clara's attempted payments. When they hired Oliver to work on Saturdays, Harry Kellar urged his son to ask half the pay he would have earned from someone else. Alex, taking over the Saturday chores when Oliver enlisted, received the same advice. "Those ladies have a hard time of it. They used to have chickens, but between hawks and foxes and weasels they lost every one. Poor old souls. In that cold house all alone. Not even an old rooster to keep them company anymore."

Oliver had continued his father's custom of taking three or four fish to the house every weekend. He'd tried several times to dig up the yard for the women, to plant potatoes and beans, but, as he complained at the supper table, "Nothing grows there but rocks, and I mean rocks. Rocks big as Alex's head."

Both women had wept the day Oliver had informed them he'd be going into the army. Old Clara insisted Rosie dig about in the upstairs bedroom for a small teakwood box described in detail by the old woman, who often forgot her own name. Who, on certain mornings, forgot to fill her mouth with her dentures or, on certain evenings, forgot to remove them. She enjoyed the comedy so much she was forever admitting the fact to friends who brought her soups or casseroles or cakes.

Rosie placed the teakwood box in her mother's lap. The old woman lifted the lid and unwrapped several layers of velvet to remove a piece of whalebone no larger than her little finger. The carved dolphin, smiling, had been inherited by her father from his grandfather. Oliver now wore the talisman on the same silver chain that contained his dog tags.

Was Oliver wearing it now in Belgium? If he was in Belgium. The 101st had been mentioned as a counterforce at the Bulge, but maybe Oliver hadn't been with his men at the time. He did make trips to rest camps occasionally, so maybe he'd been at one of the camps when the division had been called up. Wherever he was, he sure wouldn't have time to write letters now.

During the past year Alex had read his letters from Oliver to the Kilroys. Three times they'd offered him

46

letters they had received. Would he, even though they had read the letters several times, read them aloud? Sharing those letters convinced them that they were three members of a select society.

Several evenings this fall and winter, Rosie'd had cookies and hot chocolate ready when Alex arrived. They sat in front of the iron stove and talked about Oliver. Old Clara, clearheaded and often cackling like a clown, related stories about the old days, when Pequod was the most prominent fishing village in all of New England.

Alex returned from Joe Critchlow's store, hoping he'd find his mother and father smiling. His father noticed the duplicate newspapers he carried. "Why'd you buy all those newspapers?"

"Rosie Kilroy called yesterday. She asked me to bring her copies."

"The *New York Times*? The *Globe*?"

"That's what she asked for."

"Why, I'll be blessed. They haven't read any paper but the *Courier-Journal* since I was a kid. Read every word, four or five times. Anything in the papers? I'm guessin' you looked already."

"Nothing. Anything new on the radio?"

"Not yet. What about us just takin' a break collectin' our loads today?"

"Yeah. I'd rather stay home and hear the news. Are you worried, Dad?"

"Yep."

There was a knock at the front door. From his bedroom Alex could hear his father talking with someone and then his father's footsteps on the stairs.

"There's someone downstairs who wants to talk to you."

"I bet it's Larry."

His father preceded him down the stairs.

"Alex, this is Patrick Healy. He's an agent from the Federal Bureau of Investigation. Mr. Healy, this is my son Alex."

The red-haired, blunt-chinned Mr. Healy lost no time. "Alex, I know Chief Burnham already talked to you, and I know you described everything that happened. Both you and your friend." He had to refer to his notebook. "Lawrence Cobb. I just left the Cobbs' residence. Lawrence and I had a nice long chat. I'd like to ask you a few more questions."

"Sure."

How had he managed to sound so sure of himself when the floor was sliding out from beneath him? His mother and father, near the Christmas tree at the window, could have turned their heads and seen through the window what he was seeing: the *Iris* secured at the dock and, beyond the *Iris*, a fleet of fishing boats of all sizes. His mother and father seemed anxious, and Lucy, still in her fuzzy blue bathrobe, did not look too happy. Normally she would not permit herself to be seen "in such a mess," as she would put it, by any but her closest relatives.

Mr. Healy cleared his throat. When he tried a smile, neither the effort nor the eventual smile seemed sincere. He was an older man, perhaps the age of Harry Kellar, and he'd probably been a G-man a long time. He was so sure of himself, so much in charge, but his fingertips, feeling for the pages of his notebook, betrayed his nervousness. After nodding to Ethyl Kellar for permission and receiving it, he dropped into a chair at the table, which still held a few breakfast dishes. His pen, between thumb and forefinger, remained poised.

In response to the first few questions, Alex described his discovery of the body exactly as he'd described it to Chief Burnham.

Mr. Healy held up his hand, like a traffic cop stopping an oncoming car. "You sure you didn't find anything in the sand?"

"Like the other shoe? No sir. We both looked around, but we didn't find it."

"I mean something else. Not a shoe. A wallet."

Could Mr. Healy see or hear the rush of blood into his face? "No sir. There was no wallet."

"Are you certain, Alex? Lawrence Cobb remembered a wallet in the sand."

Immediate and complete relief. And satisfaction.

Relief at his ability to perceive the agent's crude attempts at deceit, satisfaction at his own ability to remain cool, possessed. If Larry had talked to the man about a wallet he could not have had the imagination to lie, he could not have thought to say they'd found it in the sand.

"Mr. Healy, there was no wallet in the sand."

Alex's firm but courteous defiance brought relief to his mother's face. His father smiled, satisfied. Lucy's admiration was so obvious that he wanted to blurt out, "You're wrong! Don't trust me! There *was* a wallet!"

But Mr. Healy followed up, too fast and too hard.

"What about a hat? Was there a hat? Any suitcase? An overnight bag?"

Harry Kellar stepped forward. "Mr. Healy, if there had been a hat or a suitcase, Alex would have said so before. I think Alex has told you everything he knows. If you don't mind, we'd like to fix our lunch now."

Mr. Healy assured Harry Kellar he had no doubts about Alex's loyalty. He did not resist when Alex's father guided him, by the elbow, to the door. "Sometimes a person has to have his memory jarred, has to be shocked into remembering forgotten facts. I've been with the bureau twenty-four years, and I've seen—"

"I'll tell you what, Mr. Healy. If my son tells me anything, I'll call you immediately."

"Would you do that?"

"You bet I will."

After Mr. Healy reached the sidewalk and got into his car and drove off, Lucy grabbed Alex and hugged

49

him. "Don't be mad, Alex. That FBI agent was only doing his duty."

Ethyl Kellar said *their* duty was to have some lunch. And then, because these were very special days and they needed all the strength they could find, they might return to church for the afternoon sermon. Would anyone object?

"I'm supposed to deliver the papers to the Kilroys, but I guess I can do that after church."

Alex sat through the hymns and the sermon—"Personal and National Despair During the Celebration of the Birth of the Christ Child"—in doleful silence. He would have been feeling better about his composure had his father not rushed to his defense so strongly. None of them could know that the agent's suspicions were justified. If his father learned the truth, he would be more humiliated than angry. His mother and Lucy would simply refuse to believe it, truth or not.

If he'd only stayed and retrieved the wallet last night. He could have produced it before the agent had had any reason to bring it up. Now he didn't dare produce it, with or without the money. Worst of all, he'd never be able to admit to anyone, not even to Oliver, that there had been a wallet and that he'd concealed it.

Something else, a question he couldn't answer. Did the FBI suspect him? Why had the FBI sent an agent to question him and Larry after both boys had been hailed as heroes not once but twice? Would they be following him now, suspecting he might lead them to the saboteurs?

As Rev. Haverford spoke of the responsibility of every man, woman, and child to fight despair, to demand hope, to pray for strength and guidance, Alex had, in this house of worship, a revelation. His country was at war. His brother might die, he might already be dead. The dead man on the beach had been a saboteur,

50

one of the enemy. There were other saboteurs roaming the countryside. That wallet—he had a vision of the Social Security card, of the driver's license, of the photographs, of other papers he'd not unfolded—could possibly help capture the Nazi saboteurs.

Once he had the wallet, he'd stuff it with ten or fifteen dollars from his newspaper savings. He'd hide it securely under a rock so it would not be washed out to sea. Someone would find it, he'd see to that. It could be one of the kids still searching the rocks every day or one of the agents who all but used a comb on the sand.

"And now," Rev. Haverford said, "let us pray."

When they left the church the Cobb family, except for Larry, marched ahead of the Kellars. Mrs. Cobb had combed her hair and wore a new black hat. "Doesn't she look pretty?" Ethyl Kellar whispered. Larry waited for Alex, and they followed the others through the door and into the vestibule.

A low voice, almost a whisper. "That agent come to your house, Alex?"

"Yeah. Yours too. He told me. Did you tell him there was a wallet in the sand?"

Larry gasped and covered his mouth with a chapped hand, the red scales making his flesh look like the side of a fish. "He lied. He's an FBI agent and he lied. J. Edgar Hoover would kill him."

"I didn't believe him. I knew you didn't tell him anything. But we have to talk. You and me."

"Pap and me are gonna buy a tree today. How about tonight?"

"Want to come by after supper?"

"Yeah, but don't expect me to eat."

They promised to support each other no matter how many FBI agents questioned them. They would continue to deny the existence of a wallet. Outside, the Kellars and the Cobbs were wishing each other a merry Christmas. They were all stomping their feet and blow-ing vaporized ice into each other's faces. Larry came close enough to Alex for Alex to see his eyes blinking, his lips quivering. "All the other kids would have believed that agent," Larry said. "You're a good friend, Alex."

Alex bumped Larry with a shoulder, and, when the impact failed to move him, he stepped on Larry's foot, and, when that too had no effect, he punched him twice, inside his open jacket. Larry giggled. "I'm getting a new jacket for Christmas, one with a zipper. See you, Alex."

Four o'clock. Alex arrived at the Kilroy house carrying the newspapers Rosie had requested. Rosie, bundled in scarves and shawls and sweaters, with a pair of oversized galoshes on her feet, picked her way carefully down the hazardous stairway as Alex came through the gate. He gave a guarded glance at the iron drum. The heavy screwdriver he carried in his pocket would break through that ice in a few seconds.

Rosie seemed apologetic, almost submissive, as she accepted the papers and picked in her ancient coin purse. She gave him the money, mumbling something about the *Courier-Journal* and the bottom landing and hot chocolate, but he couldn't understand her. Before he could ask her anything, she whirled and hurried away.

On the way back, passing the iron drum, Alex could not help turning and making sure Rosie had not stumbled. Rosie's face was framed in the kitchen window. She was watching him. She waved but remained in the window, watching. Tonight, Alex decided. No matter what, he'd get the wallet tonight. Right after dark. Then he'd take it to the shore and find the most secure site to hide it.

He'd place it high, beyond the reach of the tides. The police or the Highway Patrol or the FBI searched the area every day. One of them would find it. After its long bath in the iron drum it would be soaked. Perfect.

Tonight.

5

On the six o'clock news, the first report out of every radio station in the country was that on the evening of December 13 a German submarine had surfaced a few miles off Montauk Point, in Long Island Sound. The submarine had dispatched two rubber dinghies, each containing three men. Within seventy-two hours the three members of one dinghy had been apprehended in a so-called "safe house" on Long Island, a few miles from Brookhaven, where secret war research was being conducted.

> . . . the FBI has found caches of dynamite and explosive devices in the house, as well as maps of Long Island and New Mexico, with detail maps of New London, Connecticut, and two different cities in New Mexico. Also found were timetables for the Long Island railway system, as well as the Southern Pacific and Santa Fe railroads. A variety of schedules for buses traveling throughout New England and also the Southwest were well thumbed, with notes in the margins. Of most concern were maps of ten major rail terminals in the United States, including Buffalo, New York City, Chicago, Pittsburgh, Cleveland, and Los Angeles . . .

The FBI had offered no details to the news services about the long hours of intense investigation that had resulted in the apprehension of the three men, but the bureau did say that all three Germans possessed forged identity papers.

On a different station an enterprising investigative reporter said that there was little doubt that the man whose body had been discovered on the coast in Connecticut by two boys from a small town called Pequod was one of the Germans from the second dinghy. If that was true, there were still two saboteurs running free, perhaps in the area where the dead man had been discovered.

"What do you think of that, sweetie? You and Larry caught a Nazi." Lucy clapped her hands and would have rushed to hug Alex had he not escaped into the kitchen.

"A dead Nazi," his father added.

The words, like tiny pellets of poison, lodged in Alex's stomach, dissolved in his bloodstream, circulated through his heart into his brain. A Nazi.

Nazi.

Spy.

Saboteur.

That did it. He had to retrieve that wallet. Now. Once he had it in his hands, he'd deliver it to Chief Burnham. The chief would call the FBI. The FBI would capture the two Germans. It would all be over.

Follow-up commentaries on a variety of stations indicated that both rubber dinghies had been directed to land on Montauk, but the treacherous currents the night the submarine had surfaced had carried one of the dinghies to the shores of Connecticut. All citizens living on the East Coast, from Maine to Delaware, were urged to be alert for the appearance of strangers on the roads, the trains, the buses, as well as in automobiles.

. . . in Belgium the German attack is continuing, although two military experts interviewed by this commentator wonder if the advance has not already been blunted. German

strike units . . . brave Americans . . . This is London reporting . . .

"Can I go over to Larry's?"

"You don't want to listen to the news?"

"I've heard the news, Mom."

"A half hour," Ethyl Kellar said.

Alex nodded. He should be able to accomplish the mission in less than a half hour.

Alex had to struggle to make progress through the still unpacked snow. The McCaffreys' house was dark, but he knew the lights were on inside. Their blackout curtains were working perfectly. As were the curtains at the Kilroys' house. Not a bit of light escaped the black rectangles that were windows.

He scooped out handfuls of snow from the drum before he could effectively use the screwdriver on the ice. As he worked he chopped harder, faster, until something—he thought it was a falling branch—struck him on the side of his head, knocking him to his knees. But the branch, which continued to strike him, was uttering a mix of squeaks and squeals. And words. When Alex raised his arms to protect his face and head, the blows stopped.

Rosie Kilroy towered above him, a broom raised over her shoulder, prepared for another blow. As dark as it was, he could distinguish her eyes and her gleaming teeth, her hair spread out from her head. "I warned you. What are you doing here? I warned you." She paused to catch her breath. "I warned you," she said again, her voice a harsh, husky whisper. He could hear her wheezing.

Sobbing, and with unexpected strength, she dragged Alex to his feet, continuing to shake him. His feet slipped in the snow as he tried to stay upright, but he could not keep his balance. She pulled, dragged him, up the steps. The door was opened by someone inside before they reached the landing, and Rosie hurled Alex through the open door into the kitchen. He tumbled across the floor, bumping a chair and knocking it over, then falling himself near the table at which he'd sat so many times. He and Oliver. Eating cookies, drinking hot chocolate, talking about chickens and firewood and vegetable gardens. The door slammed behind him.

A voice on a radio in the kitchen was describing the news about the Battle of the Bulge.

When Alex finally untangled himself from his jacket and scarf and sat up, he saw two women, neither of them Rosie or Old Clara. They stood over him, each holding a revolver inches from his head, pointing at his face.

One of the women lifted him as if he were weightless, and the other ran her hands up and down his body, in and out of every pocket. The shorter, stockier of the two women, who had so thoroughly and brusquely searched him, asked, in a deep voice, "You are certain this is the boy?"

"Yes." Alex could hardly hear Rosie. She seemed to be stifling sobs or sniffling. She shouldn't have been out in the cold. She'd probably been filling the bucket with coal. "He wouldn't stay away," she said.

"Are you alone?" This from the taller woman, whose thin face was tightly drawn out to the point of her nose. Her voice was heavy, mannish.

"I'm alone."

"Do your parents know you have come here?"

"I told them I was going to Larry Cobb's house."

"Cobb," Rosie said. "The other boy in that photograph."

"I told them I'd be home in half an hour," Alex said. "I have school tomorrow. I have to go to bed early."

"You don't have school," the short woman said. "You are on vacation."

The lie had come into his head at the same time he

realized that these women were men and these men were the saboteurs who had survived the evacuation of that slashed dinghy they'd found in the sand. That explained Rosie's behavior.

Old Clara, sitting in her wheelchair near the iron stove, was observing Alex through eyes that were almost closed. Her toothless gums chewed on themselves relentlessly, and she appeared as oblivious to his arrival as she was to the heat the iron stove was sending through the room.

Should he rush for the door and speed down the stairs and zigzag across the yard and get home and call the police? Would these women-men dare kill him?

"Do not try," the short man said. He spoke unaccented English. "Miss Rose, you better tell the boy."

The shorter of the two men appeared to be in charge. He was also more relaxed, even placing his revolver on a table just slightly out of Alex's reach. The tall, hawk-nosed man remained standing, his revolver nudging Alex's forehead.

Rosie knelt at the side of the wheelchair. Oliver had made that chair from a collection of gears and wheels and pieces of sailcloth stored in the boat shed. It could be maneuvered with ease, could be spun about on itself, could tilt and lock, and, as Old Clara had marveled on its presentation, "It can do everything 'cept talk, and I bet if I tried, it'd do that." Old Clara was wrapped in several sweaters despite the red glow of the iron stove and the shimmering heat waves. Her lower legs were covered with men's wool socks, and her slippers were so worn they did not cover much more than the soles of her feet. Slumped down in her chair, she seemed unaware that Rosie had come to her to resettle her sweaters. When she suddenly chuckled, Rosie murmured, "It's all right, Momma. Do you remember Alex? Alex has come to visit us. Isn't that nice, Momma?" She turned to the shorter man. "Can I take her into her bedroom, please? She doesn't have to be out here, does she? Please?"

The tall man began what was sure to grow into a curse, or a threat, but a wave of the short man's hand silenced him. He, the short man, made a barely perceptible gesture with his head, and the tall man, reluctant but obedient, pushed the old woman and her wheelchair into a room on the left, the room Alex knew to have been Old Clara's bedroom for as long as he had been coming to the house. The tall German closed the door, then opened it, leaving enough of a gap so the old woman, as well as Rosie, who had followed them into the room, remained in sight.

"Miss Rose, come back and explain to the boy," the short man said.

"All right. Alex, these men are—"

"I know who they are. They're Germans. They're the saboteurs off that submarine."

The short man smiled. "You are one of the boys who found my friend's body."

"Yes, I found him. They'll find you too. You can't get away. The FBI caught your buddies. Your buddies squealed."

The German smiled serenely, indulgently, through the outburst. "You are famous, a patriot, twice. If I let you free, you will report us, of course. As you should."

Alex would do exactly that, but he knew better than to admit it. But what could he say that might convince these men they could trust him? The short man continued to observe him, continued to smile at him. The tall man spoke in rapid German. When the short man raised his hand for silence, the other, as if a button had been pushed to halt the current activating his voice, stopped talking. "Miss Rose," the short man said, "tell the boy."

"Alex." And Rosie inhaled deeply, preparing herself for the telling of a long story. "They came here the night the rubber boat landed. They were in that boat too. Their friend had fallen in the water. It was dark and they couldn't find him. They waited all night at the rocks. When it began to get light, they ran up the hill. This was the last house. They broke in. Now they're staying here. And you can't tell anyone. Not anyone."

"And why do we stay here?" the German asked. He sounded like a teacher quizzing a backward student.

Rosie helped him. "They're staying until emotions cool down, Alex."

"And why did you bury our clothing, Miss Rose?"

"So it wouldn't be found if someone came to search the house."

"Very good, Miss Rose. Now please tell Alex why he won't betray our presence here and why you won't betray us when you go to the store by yourself. *If* you go to the store by yourself."

"If I say a word to anyone, if the police come here, they'll kill Momma, Alex."

"Would you sacrifice your dear mother, Miss Rose? Would you let anyone know that two demon Germans are hiding in your house, holding your dear mother hostage?"

"Never. I swear."

"Commendable. Now, my young Alex, what do we do with *you*? Dieter?"

The tall, hawk-nosed German almost snapped to attention. "We cannot afford to let the boy return home. He will call the police immediately. But we cannot—"

"We cannot kill him. You are correct, Dieter. Is Dieter not correct, Alex? You are a patriotic young American. You must help your country win the war against the bestial Nazis. Correct?"

"The bestial Nazis," Dieter said, grinning, "who are now proving the weakness of the American soldier."

The short German, shaking his head, winced. He said something in German, and then, to Alex, he said, "Dieter too is a patriot."

"Oh please, Alex." Rosie peered over her hands, the

palms together as if in prayer. "You won't tell. You can't, Alex. You know how Momma loves you and Oliver. You won't tell, will you, Alex?"

Old Clara could be heard weeping in her bedroom. When Dieter saw her struggling to get out of the wheelchair, his long strides took him into the room in a few seconds. Rosie rushed after him. When they finally had Old Clara back in the chair and securely strapped, Rosie brushed back her mother's hair. She tucked another blanket around the heavily stockinged legs. Dieter returned to the living room, opened the stove's door, and deposited a large chunk of coal in the flames. He closed the hot metal door with the tip of a forefinger. The burning flesh sent out a slight sweet scent, but he did not grimace or shake his hand to relieve the pain.

"Dieter?"

"It is dangerous to release him, more dangerous to keep him. His family will miss him. They will call the police. You are expected home soon?"

"Yes," Alex said. He was shivering. His teeth began chattering. A chill crawled up his spine, reached his hair, ate into his skull. They would kill him if they could. But they didn't dare. Not tonight. But what would they do? Torture him? His eyes considered the door again.

"Do not try to escape," the short German advised him. "Then we should *have* to kill you. How old are you?"

"Fourteen."

"This old woman in the bedroom, she has been kind to you and to your brother?"

"Yes, they've both been kind. Rosie and Old . . . and Clara."

"Do you want to be responsible for the death of an old lady who's been kind to you? And for her daughter, Miss Rose? You will be responsible for their deaths if you tell anyone—*any*one—we are here."

"I won't tell."

Oliver had asked him to take care of the two old women. No one else would, so he had to. His father had assured Oliver that he'd help Alex, seeing to it that the house remained well stocked with food and firewood, but he couldn't care for two families.

"I'll do whatever you tell me to," Alex told the two men.

Rosie was weeping. "He means it, Alex. He does, he does." Her hands wiped at her eyes and then at her nose.

"I promise I won't tell anyone. I don't want them to die."

From the wheelchair came Old Clara's voice, clear and calm. "Alex, where have you been? You haven't visited us for months. Is Oliver home yet?"

Rosie, sniffling, ran to silence her mother. She returned pushing the wheelchair, so her mother could see Alex.

The short German smiled and winked at his comrade. "I believe him, Dieter. I think we can trust him. He will be our ally. Alex, you will be your enemy's ally."

Dieter snapped his fingers to catch Alex's attention. "You should know," Dieter said, "should you tell anyone we are here, we will kill not just *die Alte* but we will kill your Miss Rose as well. You would be responsible for the death of both of these women, your friends. Do you understand?"

"*Die Alte*," the short man said, "means the old one."

Alex placed a hand on Old Clara's shoulder. He managed to let the edge of his palm just barely touch the flesh of Rosie's hand. "I understand."

Dieter, as if still uncertain, said, "Observe." He reached into his pocket, withdrew a long, thin knife. A blade perhaps six inches long sprang free from the shaft. He caught a fistful of Old Clara's hair and drew it back, stretching her skinny neck taut. He touched the cutting edge of the blade to her skin.

A thin, keening whisper came from Rosie, from behind her clenched fists, now stuffed into her mouth.

Old Clara did not make a sound, but her eyes rolled up in their orbits.

Alex held his breath. His heart pumped against his ribs, blood shot up into his skull. He thought he was going to faint. "I won't tell anyone. I promise. I promise. Honest." He held out both hands to Dieter. "Please don't hurt her." He heard himself saying *"sir."*

6

Alex unbuckled his galoshes before he opened the door. Standing inside, on the hooked rug, he slipped off the galoshes and leaned outside so the snow would fall on the porch when he knocked them together.

After he removed his cap and jacket and scarf, shook the snow off them, and draped them on the rack, Alex moved brusquely to the entrance of the living room, intending to show himself and then hurry up the stairs before he could be questioned.

Harry, with Ethyl sitting beside him on the sofa, pulled his watch from his pocket. He snapped the case open. Lucy was knitting a scarf, and Tony, juggling papers, was trying to compute the week's expenses. Behind the sofa the Christmas tree blinked red and blue. Gift-wrapped boxes that had not been present before now were piled neatly on top of the white bed sheet that represented snow under the tree. Harry reached over and reduced the volume on the radio.

The blue and black ribbons, Alex noticed, had been moved. That bulge representing the German armies was now more than a bulge, it was a long extension, a black fist on the end of a long black wrist punching into the white mass of the Allied armies.

"You're a half hour late."

"I'm sorry, Dad." A lie formed itself, but before he spoke it Alex had the sense that everything inside him as well as all about him was collapsing. The lie was ready so easily, so quickly.

He'd rushed out of the Kilroys' house when the short German had considered him seriously committed to secrecy. He'd run as fast as he could down the dangerously slippery stairway and through the snow-covered yard and past the McCaffreys' house. He'd not thought about staying, or returning after the door had been closed, to dig at the ice again, to get the wallet. Now, standing in his own home, the wallet seemed insignificant. The only important fact in his life was the trap he found himself in. He, Alex Kellar, was the only person in the entire country who knew where those German spies were hiding, and he could do nothing about it. Nothing nothing nothing!

They were all looking at him as if special effort was required to recognize this stranger who'd just tumbled into the house from the snowstorm outside.

Another lie. "I'm sorry. Larry and I were listening to the news." The lie could not be checked because the Cobbs didn't have a phone.

He choked over the lump inside his throat. Tears charged up into his eyes. He ran up the stairs, wanting to hurl himself not just beneath the blankets but beneath the bed. If it were only possible to burrow deeper, into the floor and down through the house and into the cellar.

He heard Rosie's plea again; he saw Old Clara's chin stretched up, her eyes white, as the knife blade touched her throat. So frightened, so helpless. They depended on him. They trusted him. He'd promised them he would tell no one.

Halfway up the stairway his stockinged feet slipped on the carpeted steps, and he fell, tumbling back down to the landing. He sobbed not because his head had struck the banister but because . . . why? He didn't want to know.

He heard them—his mother, father, Lucy, Tony—

speaking at the same time. Then he was in Tony's arms, and his mother and father were prodding his arms and legs. Are you all right, Alex? . . . Oh, your head, it's bleeding . . . The Hundred First will fight free, Alex. In a week or two Oliver will be reading your letters . . . He'll be reading about you in those *Courier-Journal* stories . . . We know why you're so upset, but you have to be brave, brave as Oliver . . .

Harry Kellar took Alex into his own arms and carried him up the stairs as he'd carried him when he'd been a baby. Ethyl followed. Lucy, weeping, remained on the bottom landing with Tony, calling to Alex to sleep well, to have pleasant dreams. Tony promised that next Friday he'd find some extra gas and they'd take Alex with them to a movie in New London.

After tucking him in, Ethyl and Harry sat on the bed. Their being here with him must have been a step back in time for them too. Alex tried to be matter-of-fact as his mother leaned over to kiss him. Even his father demonstrated an unusual sentimentality. His voice, as he glanced at Alex and then at the photographs above the desk, was tender, saying, "You're growing so fast, but you're not a man yet, thank God."

"You're still my boy," his mother said. "You're alone so much. I ought to stay home more."

"We both stay away too much," his father added. "We work all day at Electric Boat, and we're too tired at night to do anything but eat and listen to the news and spot airplanes."

"The volunteering." And Ethyl looked to Harry, as if he might help her here. "I think we could ease off some. We've done it for years. Let someone else, the younger . . ."

But Harry was shaking his head. "You gotta do what you gotta do. Everyone's tired. But with the troops over there, fighting, here at home we can't give up just because we're sleepy."

"I'm not lonely," Alex said. "It's Christmas and there's a war and Olly's fighting over there and . . . I wish this war was over."

"We do, too, Alex." His mother sighed. Words, the shake of her head implied, were just not adequate to describe her worries. "Didn't we agree we'd try to have a good old-fashioned Christmas?"

"I didn't get anyone presents."

"That's all right." His father left the bed. His mother followed him to the door. They both turned to smile for him.

"Christmas is for the young," Ethyl said. "You're home. That's our sweetest gift. Good night, Alex."

As his father's hand rested on the light switch, Alex heard him promise. "Sunday, Alex. Next Sunday morning. We'll take out the *Iris*. Maybe we'll take lunch with us. And we'll do some fishing." After he turned off the light but before he closed the door, Harry cleared his throat. "It's going to be a fine Christmas, Alex. I feel it in my bones."

Alex called the darkness in. He wanted it to envelop him. Somewhere in the vicinity of the wall he saw, through the darkness, Oliver surrounded by German soldiers, Oliver being shot.

To flee the scene he chose the darkness beneath the comforter.

Christmas morning.

There were the usual greetings and cries of surprise and pleasure about the wrappings and the gifts, and then the thank-yous. But there was no denying the air of dread that squeezed around that familiar joy that had colored all previous Christmas mornings.

Everyone managed to keep the radio silent until after all the gifts were opened and all the nuts and fruits were sampled and, finally, most of the biscuits and jam and scrambled eggs and slices of bacon and ham were consumed, along with the rationed coffee held in reserve for this very morning.

Then Harry Kellar, unable to resist any longer, turned on the radio, but he was considerate enough to keep the voices of the reporters no louder than a murmur in the background.

And then, because there was a war on, because this year Christmas day was like any other day for the defense industry, as it was for all the fighting forces, Alex's mother and father packed their metal boxes with sandwiches and thermoses of coffee and made their way to the bus that would deliver them to New London and Electric Boat.

Lucy and Tony went for a Christmas morning walk, inviting Alex to join them, but Alex said no, he wanted to stay home and look through some of the books he'd received as gifts.

After Lucy and Tony left Alex stared at the radio. Did he want to hear the news? Before he had to make a decision, he was rescued by a knock on the front door.

There was Larry, wearing a new pair of high-tops that had been smeared with grease so they'd be waterproof.

"Come in," Alex said. "You want some breakfast?"

"No. I couldn't sleep. I knew you'd be up."

"There's lots left."

Larry did not refuse the second invitation. In fact, he picked two more slices of toast from the plate and another glass of milk, after he finished the last scrap of eggs. He attacked the food as if it were the meanest kid at school.

Alex watched the food disappear. "I bet you didn't eat before you left home."

"I did so. But just once." Larry stretched out his legs to display the greased high-tops. "A Christmas present. My galoshes were worn out. Neat, huh? At first it took me three minutes to lace up each one. I got it down to two minutes now." He scraped up the crumbs and scraps from all the plates on the table and spooned them into his mouth. "What's wrong, Alex? You look like you're sick. You have the flu? All my sisters got it. Not me. I'm too healthy. It's goin' 'round, Pap says. You sure look like you got it."

"I'm trying to think."

Larry, not easily wounded, was not impressed by Alex's irritation. Like all the Cobbs, Larry seemed to have inherited the ability to remain immune from scorn or hostility. Having devoured all the crumbs, he wet a fat forefinger and, with the tip, wiped every plate and bowl. He sucked the thin paste from his finger with a loud smack. "Another ten days vacation," he said. "Pap's gonna get a job at Electric Boat. Mom, too. Pap says you get used to havin' money. We'll get a phone. Then you and me can talk at night. That money, boy it sure changed our life. Hey, you look like you're gonna bawl. Your eyes are all scrunched up and wet and you look like—"

"Larry, you're so stupid you don't know your foot from your hand."

Alex pushed his chair back, ran up the stairs to the bathroom, and stayed there for at least fifteen minutes. Then he went into his bedroom, to stand and stare at the bed before putting the sheets and the comforter and pillows into a semblance of order. When he returned to the kitchen to wash the dishes, he refused to respond to Larry's call from the living room. The radio was crackling and buzzing as Larry turned the knob.

"There's a station somewhere that only plays cowboy songs. I heard Sons of the Pioneers last night. They sang 'Cool Water.' It's about tryin' to find water in the desert and talkin' to your horse." Larry, trying to remember the words, came up with two, plus several hums, and did no better with the tune.

"Larry, I have to tell you something." Alex stopped sloshing about in the sink. He seemed preoccupied with the suds and the way the froth broke into bubbles that rode the surface and then popped. "But you have to promise, scout's honor, cross your heart, you won't say anything to anyone."

Larry was much more interested in the offer to trust him with a secret than he was in the cowboy music. He rarely received offers of trust or confidence, of sharing of secrets, and to get such an offer from his best friend—actually his only friend—assured excitement. He waited, silent, wide-eyed, expectant.

"Promise?"

"Sure I promise. Did I ever turn on you, Alex? Remember the G-man and the promise we made? I kept my promise, didn't I?"

"That was yesterday, not even one day ago. Can you keep a promise forever?"

Forever. The promise of such eternal trust seemed to puff up Larry's body beyond its usual size and shape. "Hey, Alex, I promise. What is it?" After struggling to break free from the sofa's cushions, he finally made it. He swaggered into the kitchen, his face flushed. He dipped his head, urging Alex on.

Alex tried to decide where to begin. He heard again the hysterical voice of Rosie, he saw the knife blade against Old Clara's stretched throat. He recalled his own promise to both women. *I won't tell anyone.*

"I can't tell you, Larry."

Larry's heavy fist struck the sink, the drainboard, shaking two washed cups back into the soapy water. "That's not fair!" He hurled himself toward the door, grabbing his jacket from the rack on the way. Right hand on the doorknob, he delayed his departure long enough to ask, "You gonna tell me?"

"I can't, Larry. I shouldn't have said I'd tell you. I'm sorry."

Larry tore open the door, stepped into the shrieking wind, and slammed the door behind him. Then the door opened just enough to permit the entry of his head. "Last chance. You gonna tell me?"

When Alex continued washing the dishes, offering nothing, Larry slammed the door again and thumped his way across the porch and down the steps.

After he swept the kitchen and dried the dishes and returned them to their cupboards, Alex went upstairs, to move in and out of his room and Lucy's room and his parents' room. Downstairs again, he went from kitchen to living room to dining room to the windows at the back, the windows at the front. He could not sit still for fear of something, something sinister—a person, an animal, a force—coming up behind him and grabbing and choking him.

On the sofa he clicked the radio switch. Exhausted, sick, choked by a sudden, heavy nausea, he lay back and not so much slept as passed out. Sometime later he stood, wandered into the kitchen, drank some milk directly from the bottle, and wondered if writing a letter to Oliver might not clear his mind. He sat at the desk, but instead of writing he talked to the photographs. It was only after some time that he remembered he had to pick up his papers.

The fifty-one copies of the *Courier-Journal* fitted loosely into the canvas bag. Standing at the distribution dock, Alex scanned the front page of the demo copy tacked to the bulletin board. GERMANS CONTINUE ADVANCE—ALLIED TROOPS RESIST!

The iron drum was almost filled with snow again. Alex veered close as he passed it, thinking about the wallet for the first time since yesterday. It was no longer worth his efforts to locate it. Events had passed it by. Maybe later.

He intended to throw the paper from the gate, then run off before they could get him into the house. If he stayed away long enough, there was some chance he'd come up with a plan for getting the men captured without endangering Rosie and her mother.

Rosie must have been watching for him. She came onto the upstairs landing. "You have to come in, Alex. You have to."

He had no choice. No telling what they'd do if he refused. As he trudged up the stairs, he noticed that each step had been swept clear of snow. Rosie held the door for him and closed it after he entered.

The two men, still dressed as women, were sitting at the kitchen table. And the radio was on, the voice loud.

. . . The One Hundred First Airborne had been advancing on Bastogne for almost twenty-four hours. Now dug in, the men of the One Hundred First are facing encirclement by German armored divisions. The Germans are determined to take Bastogne, the One Hundred First is determined to hold it . . .

Alex tried to remember where the pin representing the 101st was stuck in his father's large wall map. But Dieter's comment —"I give them six hours"— brought him back to this room.

The surface of the oak table, having endured hundreds of scourings with lye soap, by Rosie as well as her mother, was almost white. A large pot bubbled away on top of the stove, and something—a chicken, perhaps—was sending herbed aromas from the oven. The tall, hawk-nosed German went from window to window to observe the terrain. "It's clear," he said. "He came alone."

"Of course he did. He said he would. Alex is a man of his word, as we say in America. Correct, Alex?" The shorter man, at the table, had been carving a block of wood. His lap was filled with shavings, and there was a fair-sized pile of shavings on the floor. He was using one broad-bladed knife. A second knife, with a slender blade, lay on the table.

"I have to go right home. They're expecting me."

The wood-carver held up his hand. "Not so fast, my

friend." He ignored the snort of contempt from the tall man at the window.

"Your father owns a boat. The *Iris*. Correct?"

"I told him," Rosie explained. "I had to."

The tall man ordered her to be quiet and started toward her, as if preparing to reinforce his command, but the short man said something in German. His voice, though soft, must have contained authority. The tall man stiffened and returned to the windows to keep an eye on the land outside.

The German at the table stood up, letting the shavings fall to the floor. "Alex, I am Hans. He is Dieter. You should know our names if only because you must not think of us as *the tall German* or *the short German*." He smiled. "We need your help with a plan we're preparing. We will need to use the *Iris* tomorrow morning. It has a radio, I presume."

These two men sail his beloved *Iris*? The boat Oliver loved, the boat his father's father had built? No.

"The engine's not working. We haven't had her out for a month. Ask Rosie and Clara. We always bring them fish when we go out. We haven't brought them anything for a month."

"Very well. We'll examine this tomorrow morning. Dieter can repair any engine ever built, so be sure to bring fuel."

"Where will you take her? How can you take her and not be seen?" Alex wanted to say, "They'll catch you." But he held it back, thinking that his warning might just save them. He realized that once they were out on the water, he'd be free to call the police.

"*You* will take it out. Early, when everyone is sleeping. You will return to your dock at five o'clock, several hours before your parents wake up, two hours before your sister is awake. What is his sister's name again, Miss Rose?"

"Lucille."

"Lucille, yes."

"I had to tell them," Rosie wailed. And, from the bedroom, Old Clara's voice rang out clearly, angrily. "She had to. Or they'd hit her again."

"I won't help you," Alex snapped. "You hit Rosie. Do anything you want to. Go ahead, kill me. You think you won't get caught? They'll catch you. The FBI always gets their man."

"A mistake, Alex. I confess. Dieter's temper sometimes breaks out of control. It will not happen again. Unless, of course, you refuse to help us. Then I just might have to be in another room when Dieter loses his temper. Now. The engine . . . what about the engine on the *Iris*?"

"We haven't taken it out because, well, my dad works all the time. I take it out myself but only when the weather's fair."

"But you are very capable. Miss Rose says your father told her you'll be the best in the family."

"Better than his father or grandfather," Rosie said. "That's what he told me."

"Tomorrow morning at four o'clock we will meet you at the dock. You will take us out."

"There might be a storm."

"Since when is a New England fisherman frightened of a bit of foul weather? Hmm? Tell me. Four o'clock. Do you have an alarm clock?"

"I can borrow my sister's."

"No. Your sister Lucille will be suspicious. I will loan you Miss Rose's." He picked up the block of wood and began carving. "Would you care for a bowl of soup, Alex? The man at the General Store delivered food this morning. Do not look so hopeful. He did not see us. We decided Miss Rose should not be there in the store alone. I have made a fine potato soup and a roast chicken. Also bread and a kuchen. Pardon me. A cake. Would you join us?"

"He's a good cook, Alex." Rosie supplemented her praise with a rub of her stomach. "He's better than I am. Momma eats everything he makes. She's never eaten like she eats now."

"I have to go home. They're waiting for me. I was late last night, and I caught it."

"Caught it?" Dieter said.

"They were mad."

"Did they spank you?"

"Alex is much too old to be spanked," Hans said. He was not trying to be humorous when he said it, but understanding, supportive. "You shall eat with us another time."

"What if the engine doesn't start?"

Hans nodded in the direction of Dieter. "He'll start it. Miss Rose, your alarm clock for Alex?"

As he opened the door to make his way down the stairs, Alex heard Rosie's voice behind him. "Alex. Merry Christmas, Alex."

A snort and a loud sharp chuckle came from the tall German.

Evening. The gray, snow-filled sky bulged down, looking thick and heavy enough to be probed with a finger. Alex stood at the end of the dock, looking up across the now white rise of what, in a few months, would be green lawn. One of his summer jobs, as it had been Oliver's, was to keep that grass mowed. Wouldn't he love to feel the hot sun now, see the green grass, smell the summer breezes off the sea? He turned to observe the *Iris* tugging at her ropes, straining to get into deep water. Close by was the *Patsy Anne*, the Salazars' boat. Enrique Salazar had died last year in the Pacific, on some island with an unpronounceable name, charging a Japanese bunker. On the far side of the *Patsy Anne* was the *Sea Sprite*. Joe McChesney and his humpbacked son spent most of their time living aboard the *Sea Sprite* rather than at home with the other ten McChesneys. The *Rose Marie*, a delicate little thing no one had expected to survive a single winter, had brought the Cunninghams

74

a fine living for the last ten years. Out in the water, twenty or thirty feet off but still protected by the cove, were the *Poppy* and the *Crummy*, one having saved several generations of the Arnolds, the other having endured at least five generations of the Whorfs, men almost as large as the boat itself.

> Dear Alex:
> I went fishing yesterday in a German river with a pole and earthworms. Didn't catch a thing. I keep thinking about the Iris and how we used to . . .

In the morning he could pretend he'd forgotten. Or he could swear the clock had failed.

Cold as it was, Alex did not want to go inside yet. His mother and father would have returned from work. A casserole would be in the oven, waiting. Would his mother know tomorrow or the next day when she looked at his face? They would be sound asleep when he returned at five. Would they later smell the boat on his clothes? The river and the sea in his hair?

As the waves slapped the sides of the boats, he saw tomorrow's actions taking place as if they were being projected onto the screen of the Majestic Theater in town. Through half-closed eyes he watched the events progress. There they are in the *Iris*, the three of them, heading out, moving through the snow. Hans sits in the bow. Dieter sits at the stern, tiller-steering the boat into rougher water. He, Alex, stands at the wheel.

Many times, with Oliver or his father, Alex had handled the tiller in rougher seas than this, in waves that built like advancing cliffs high above the boat and then dropped like thousands of boulders hurled by giants. But the *Iris* had never faltered. Now Alex saw the *Iris* yielding to the storm, breaking up, taking them all down into the cold water.

That would be the way to beat them.

75

He could not be in combat in Europe, but he could be in combat at home, fighting the same enemy Oliver was fighting. He was the only person here at home, the only person in Pequod, Connecticut, the United States, who would be in hand-to-hand combat with the enemy. He would die as they would. But with the Germans gone from the house, Rosie could call the police.

One by one their bodies would wash ashore. There would be a funeral when his body was found. Now, on the screen, Alex saw his mother and father standing at his grave. Lucy, leaning on Tony, is weeping. Tony, in his loose, wrinkled suit, arm around Lucy's waist—even Tony is weeping.

Alex brushed the images from the screen and left the dock. But the idea persisted. He'd do it. He'd sink the *Iris* and take them all to their deaths.

He sat on the edge of the bed in which Oliver used to sleep. He gazed absently at the comforter that used to keep Oliver warm. Oliver's head had rested on that pillow. Would Oliver survive the war only to return to visit his, Alex's, grave?

. . . and when I get back we'll go out for a week.
Just the two of us, Alex. I want to feel the old Iris
slide through the water. Just you and me . . .

He went into the bathroom, let the cold water flow over his hands. The Atlantic's water would be colder. No one could survive in the Atlantic for more than ten minutes.

He shivered at the promised thrill of the rushing, icy water. Then he saw himself jumping over the rocks at the beach. There in the sand lies the man in the dark suit. Dead. Blue-faced. How long had *he* lived after he'd fallen out of the dinghy?

Alex watched the water circle as it struck the bottom of the sink and started down the drain.

7

After Alex settled the clock beneath his pillow, he tested it to be sure the alarm could be heard. He didn't want the sound traveling outside the room. Wrapped in a sweater and topped by the pillow, the clock's bell was soft but audible.

When he awoke at three thirty, his mother and father would be sound asleep. Lucy, too, would be asleep; she wouldn't wake for four or five hours. She and Tony always stayed up late, playing cards or Monopoly or Parcheesi. Tony waited until the Kellars came home, then he walked back through the snow to his flat above the Pequod Café.

By the time his father did wake up, Alex would be back in bed, asleep. No one would know that he'd been gone an hour, that he'd taken out the *Iris*, that he'd helped the two German saboteurs being hunted by police and the FBI and every amateur sleuth in Connecticut. He almost wished his mother and father did know. If they had even the slightest sense of his private, wretched world, they would come to his rescue. They'd do whatever they thought was right to do, whatever they had to do. They would make the decisions. Whatever happened to Rosie and Old Clara would be their responsibility, not his.

But that *promise* returned to haunt him. Why should a *promise* mean so much? Because Rosie had been so frightened, because she'd pleaded, because she trusted him, because she and her mother loved Oliver, because Oliver had left them in his charge, because they were old, virtually defenseless, lonely people, because they were being tortured, because they were not just friends but were somehow almost relatives. Because they were without champions to fight their cause. That was why Rosie had begged for his promise, that was why he had promised. The only thing that relieved her own terrors now was the fact that she could trust Alex not to endanger her or her mother further.

Well, there it was. He couldn't tell his parents or Lucy or Tony or Larry or the police or anyone. Would he tell Oliver if Oliver was here? Yes. Immediately.

His long johns and knitted wool sweater and watch cap came under the comforter with him so that at three thirty, when he dressed, they would be so warm his body would have no time to be chilled. Once beneath the comforter, Alex probed under the pillow, inside the sweater, to be sure the alarm lever had not been pushed to off.

Would he sleep through the alarm? There were days when he didn't hear or didn't want to hear his mother or father pounding on the door to get him up and out of the house for school. He couldn't take the chance. He didn't dare betray the two Germans. They would punish Rosie.

Movies. He'd stay awake by watching movies all night. Behind his closed eyelids, the screen of the Majestic Theater popped into view, a flat sheet of silver. It filled itself with figures, with streets and houses. Oliver appeared in full combat gear, his chin thrust into the strap of his steel helmet. Oliver listened attentively as Alex, also dressed in combat gear—as if he too was in the army—narrated the events that had led to this moment: the body at the shore, the rubber dinghy, the strange behavior of Rosie Kilroy, his meeting the two German saboteurs.

Now Oliver and Alex were teamed for an assault,

both of them holding M-1 rifles, both of them advancing across the snow, through the litter, up the stairs. Oliver led the way, and, at the landing, he gave his signal nod to Alex. Alex returned the signal. Oliver threw his body at the door and leapt inside, his rifle firing. Dieter fell first, screaming . . . Hans fell . . . no, Hans was only wounded.

It was all over. Out of the bedroom came a grateful Rosie, pushing a fist-waving Old Clara in her wheel-chair. FBI agents and photographers and reporters waited in the yard. Newspapers, twirling and zooming forward as they did in the movies, contained photographs of the two German spies, photographs of Alex and Oliver at the White House in Washington, President Roosevelt in his wheelchair reaching up to pin medals on their jackets. In the audience: his mother and father, holding hands, tears in their eyes, Lucy beaming, Tony in his crumpled suit and food-stained tie. Oh, and Larry Cobb, casting fascinated glances at the long table (be-hind President Roosevelt) covered with meats and breads and salads and creamy desserts. Outside—or was it inside?—bells were ringing.

The alarm!

Alex found the clock, turned off the alarm. Silence. He'd fallen asleep. How long had the alarm been ring-ing? Had anyone heard it? He held his breath, waited, listened. The only sound was the light wind pushing at the windows. He turned on the bedside lamp long enough to see the clock. Three thirty-five. He threw the covers aside.

Quickly now: long johns, sweater, jacket, cap, long woolen socks. He tiptoed downstairs, cautious on the fourth step, which had, for as long as he could remem-ber, squeaked at the slightest pressure. In the small room at the rear of the house, behind the kitchen, he lifted down his sea clothes. Once in boots and oilskins, he opened the back door and eased it closed, checking twice to be sure it was not locked. He did not want to be trapped outside when he returned. Only as he moved along the side of the house, head bowed against the wind-driven snow, the wall at his fingertips, did he remember that he was not returning. He was taking the two enemies into the ocean with him.

Perhaps their bodies would be found early this morning.

Near the dock, Alex glanced back. Not a window or door could be seen through the dense snowfall. His home might never have been there.

As familiar as he was with the path that led to the dock, Alex had to be careful not to step off it and into the water. Beneath his boots the snow popped like pistol shots. The boards of the dock creaked and groaned. Twenty-three steps, one foot slowly in front of the other. When he reached the point where the towline should have been available, he extended his arm. The rope was there, and there, too, was the ladder. And a voice that came from below like the voice of a swimming ghost: "Five minutes early. Good." It was Hans. "Let's go. We found the fuel in that shack."

Alex, more angry than frightened now, replied that that *shack* was the engine house. His father had built it.

"It's a shack," Dieter said.

Alex descended the ladder. The *Iris* leaned and trembled beneath the weight of his body. He said, as his feet touched the deck, "The oars are tied—"

"We have them," Hans said. "And we have a compass. Are you ready, Alex?" He didn't wait for an answer. As the boat pulled away from the dock, Alex heard the squeak of wet cloth rubbing wet cloth. They had wrapped the oar locks to stifle the noise.

A thin beam of light at the stern cut through the falling snow. It was angled downward, showing, at the edges, Hans and Dieter bent over a map. Dieter positioned the compass over the map. They exchanged murmured comments in German.

What would they be saying to him or to each other if they knew that they were going to be dead in twenty or thirty minutes? He had a vision of his own body, inside the weight of his boots and his oilskins, sinking beneath the surface.

"I'm here, Alex," Rosie said.

He thought he was imagining it, but then, squinting, he convinced himself he could see her, a fourth figure, midship. The *Iris* pushed ahead, shifting forward with each set of wet-cloth sounds. As they rowed, Rosie wept concerns for Old Clara: "Oh, Momma, what'll she . . . Be sure to . . . Momma, Alex . . ."

Why had they brought Rosie? To torture her? No. She'd surely know the coast, the small towns, where people lived. She'd been born and raised here, she could advise them. But no, they wouldn't need her advice. They'd brought her for their own protection. If anyone caught them, they would be safe with Rosie as hostage.

They were safe as well from any plan Alex might have concocted. They knew he wouldn't betray her. No, and he wouldn't sink the boat.

Dieter's voice. "We start the engines soon?"

Alex, standing at the wheel, waiting to be given directions, asked where they were going.

"New London," Hans replied.

"We better be more north by northeast. And we better not start the motor yet."

"How do you know which way we're going or must go?" Dieter asked, the usual sneer present, even in his voice. "You can't see ten feet ahead in this snow, and you don't have a compass. Just do as we say."

"I'm sure we're off. I've got a feeling."

Suspicious, curt, Dieter replied again. "Come back here and take the tiller. We'll give you directions." A fragment of the scenario Alex had created last night returned: Dieter reaching for Alex's gun, Oliver firing his M-1, Dieter falling.

"Hurry!"

Alex, clinging to the wash rail, felt his way toward the tiller. His legs brushed those of Hans, who continued to row, bending forward and drawing back without effort, without heavy breathing.

Dieter's voice ordered Rosie to move toward the bow.

"Oh please let me stay here. I've never been out at night. I'm so cold. If I fall over . . . I can't swim . . . Momma will never . . ."

Hans's gentler voice came: "You won't fall, Miss Rose. Here, give me your hand . . . there . . . now go on, keep moving up."

She moved, still sobbing quietly. When she bumped into Alex, she grabbed him, tried to cling to him. "Oh please take care of Momma, Alex."

"Hurry, Miss Rose." Hans's voice was less sympathetic.

"We better keep our voices down," Alex said. As he pulled Rosie's hands loose he murmured into her ear, "Don't worry, we'll be OK." But he could not help wondering if perhaps they'd already murdered Old Clara and were intending, when the time was appropriate, to murder him and Rosie.

Edging forward, clinging to the rail, Alex struck a cardboard box with one foot. He almost fell. His knee touched what proved to be a suitcase. And another suitcase. Both moved easily under his hands. They had to be empty. He finally reached the seat at the stern. Dieter left as soon as Alex's hand touched the wooden shaft of the tiller. "I'll take the wheel," Dieter said. "Now we use the engine."

"Not yet. They'll hear us."

Rosie was weeping again. She called out to Alex that there was food on the sink board. Her mother's lunch. There was more food in the refrigerator for her supper. "Please take care of Momma, Alex. Don't call the police."

Rosie must have known their plans. She'd heard them talk, knew where they were going, how long they'd be gone or if they'd be returning. If Alex was to feed Clara lunch, they were probably planning to be gone all day.

Dieter sounded quite pleased with himself. "That's right. Their lives are in your hands, Alex. If you want her dead, you will try to trick us."

"I promise, Rosie. I'll take care of her. I'll check your mother as soon as I get back, and I'll feed her at noon. Supper, too?"

"You are not so clever as you think," Dieter said. "You need not know when we return."

Hans must have thought Dieter's suspicions did not deserve serious consideration. "We'll be coming back this afternoon on the bus. We'll be at the house when you bring the paper. Understand?"

Up forward, Dieter pressed the starter button. The engine coughed several times. After he choked it, the engine caught. Alex gripped the tiller in frustration. Why hadn't the engine failed? But it hadn't failed, and the *Iris* was shooting ahead at, Alex guessed, three or four knots.

"Stop," Alex called, louder than he'd intended. Dieter threw the engine into reverse and gave a hard right. The *Iris* slowed, the engine idled.

"Put your hand out to starboard," Alex said. "Go to the rail and reach out."

The *Iris* rose and fell as both men did as he'd suggested. He heard a curse. It had to be a curse. In German. That was Dieter. Then brief chuckles. That was Hans. "The boy knows what he's doing. Ten seconds more and we would have crashed. What is it, Alex?"

"A fishing boat. Probably Handy Cawley's *Sea Nymph*. He never docks her. He lives aboard."

"Hallooo down there. Who's down there?" Another

call from the deck of the *Sea Nymph* was covered by two long blasts from its foghorn.

"What do we do, Alex?"

"Row forward. For five minutes. Then we can use the engine. But row easy." While Hans and Dieter rowed, Alex leaned over to trail his hand in the water, to feel the flow of the tide, the swirl of currents. "When I leave you off, what do I do? If my dad gets up early and finds me gone, the first thing he'll do is go down to the dock. He'll find the *Iris* gone, and he'll call the police. Probably the Coast Guard, too."

"Don't be too smart," Dieter said, not able to row and talk as easily as Hans was. His words had been broken for groans and grunts and deep breaths.

"After you leave us off," Hans said, "you go right back. Go to bed. Your father will find you there, and he won't suspect anything. After breakfast go to Miss Rose's house. Her mother is in bed. She is tied in. Don't worry, she's comfortable. Leave her that way."

"I put a diaper on her, Alex. I'll change her when we—"

Hans's "Quiet!" was almost as severe as Dieter could have made it.

"When will you be back? I can't go over after dark."

"We put coal in the fire this morning," Hans said, ignoring the question, or choosing to answer in his own time.

"I'm going to the café for supper. I can't go to their house after that. Dad won't let me. We'll be doing things."

"Fuel the fire at noon and . . . When do you pick up your newspapers?"

"Three o'clock."

"Good. Coal in the fire this morning. And then before you go for the newspapers. We return before dark. She won't get cold. She's covered with blankets."

"How will you get back?"

"Do not ask questions," Dieter snapped. He spoke

in German, but Hans did not respond. After a while, as if he'd been deliberating, Hans said, "We'll be at the house tonight when you bring the newspaper. Now, the net. What do you know about the net?"

Alex hadn't thought about the antisubmarine net. It had gone up within days after the United States had declared war against Germany and Japan. New London, one of the major submarine bases in the world, also employed thousands of civilians, including his mother and father. A thick steel-mesh net, stretched from bank to bank, was designed to keep out foreign vessels, and especially submarines, that might try to sail up the river. It was released and drawn open during limited daylight hours for local fishermen who had to travel to and from the ocean. It would definitely be closed now.

"The net, Alex."

"I don't know much. Dad has a special license that gets him up and down the river. I think it opens at eight."

Dieter, not asking for advice, started the engine. Every few minutes Hans used the flashlight to check the map and the compass and then give Alex directions that kept them on the course he'd selected. "Can you read a compass, Alex?"

"Sure."

"Of course you can. What young son of a New England fisherman can't read a compass? As stupid a question as asking a fourteen-year-old boy in Berlin if he knows the words to the 'Horst Wessel.' Correct, Dieter?"

Dieter seemed not to have heard.

"I will leave you our compass. Will you have trouble returning? This snow is like a thick fog."

"No. I've come here a hundred times."

"A hundred?"

"Well, fifty."

"But never alone. Correct?"

"No, never alone. But I can make it. I've been out alone before."

"On the sea?"

"About ten times."

"Meaning three or four. Or two. Once?" He laughed. "I know about boys."

Alex resolved to ease himself out of the casual banter that had been developing. He would talk only when asked a question and then would say as few words as possible. That rule was easy to establish for Dieter. Alex wouldn't be at all unhappy if he never exchanged a word with that man again. But Hans did not have a mean or threatening air about him. He even seemed interested in establishing some sort of friendship.

The light flickered. "It is twelve minutes past four o'clock," Hans said. "In six minutes the tide will be at its highest. The west end of the net will be five feet under water."

Alex gasped. "How do you know that?"

"In a space ten feet wide. We will cross over the net there, in that space near the lock. Not quite three hundred yards up the river is a shoal, a sandy beach. The only such beach along the river."

"Oyster Beach."

"Correct. Oyster Beach. We get off the boat at Oyster Beach. You will return home with the *Iris* immediately. You'll be back across the net before the tide falls enough to trap you. We kill the engine now and we row."

How did they know so much? He could understand their being informed of the net. That was common knowledge. But the tides? Well, tide charts were available for every sea in the world. Free. But how could they have known exactly where it would be safe to cross the net?

The squeaking of wet cloth on wet cloth paused. The bottom of the *Iris* scraped the top cable of the net.

"Faster," Hans said. "Row faster."

"Alex," Rosie whimpered. "Don't forget Momma."

Dieter snapped a threat in German that resulted in Rosie's quiet sobbing.

"I'll take care of Clara, Rosie."

Dieter's threat this time was directed at Alex. Safe in the darkness Alex raised his hand to his face, fitted his thumb to his nose, and waved his fingers, then slowly, quietly, but with great satisfaction, lowered his hand to his lap.

There were four flashlights in the engine room of the *Iris*. Alex needed no map, but he did need to use the compass. Alone now, he had to use the engine. He could not row alone and cover the distance before sunrise. He prayed as he pushed the starter button. The engine coughed, gasped, coughed, and then caught. The *Iris* slid over the net's top cable, picked up speed, moved out to sea. Alex fixed the compass in his lap and the flashlight next to it. He would only need to flash the light for a second or two.

Alex admitted his fatigue as the *Iris* approached the dock. He could have stretched out on the floor of the engine room and slept there, in the cold wetness, but he forced himself onto the ladder, up the rungs, onto the dock. Across the dock, up the path, across the yard. The snow rose above his knees. He fell twice but rose again and finally found himself at the back door of his home. He leaned against the sill, remembering that it was unlocked.

In the entryway he removed his boots and oilskins. He staggered across the dark kitchen without bumping a table or chair and fought his way blindly up the stairs, forgetting that telltale step. It squeaked. He stumbled on. No one appeared. He dropped on his bed and pulled the comforter about up over his chest and shoulders and head.

8

"Alex. Alex, honey. Time to get up."

Lucy's voice drew him out of the darkness. He burrowed deep, trying to recover both the warmth and the night, but the voice continued calling.

He let Lucy's arm slide under his back and raise him up. "Honey, you are absolutely unconscious. Am I gonna have to go get Tony? You're too big. I can't lift you."

He opened his eyes, looked about, almost dropped back, but then said, "OK, I'm up. I'm awake."

"Mom and Dad left early."

She was heading him toward the bathroom. "Alex, you look like you're walking in your sleep. Did you stay awake late last night? I bet you read."

"I'm just tired. Did Mom and Dad get their shifts changed?"

"They're working extra hours today and tomorrow. Special work. They need extra welders and inspectors. Mom and Dad volunteered. And I volunteered to get you your breakfast before I go to the café. Now go on in the bathroom."

He stood in the doorway, wavering. Lucy placed a hand on his forehead. "You do have a slight temperature. I think maybe you ought to stay in bed today. Tell you what. There's eggs and bacon in the fridge. You've made breakfast for yourself. You know what to do. I'll go on to the café." She led him back to bed. He followed willingly. "You're all warm and toasty now. Right? You sleep and make your own breakfast when you get up."

He shoved his hand outside the blankets to find her wrist, her hand. She squeezed his fingers and leaned down to brush his forehead with her kiss. "Everything's gonna be OK, Alex. The Germans won't take Bastogne, and Oliver will laugh when he tells us all about it. Next year we're all gonna have Christmas together. OK?"

He must have said OK in response, because a clean new silence entered the room and a warmth washed over him as the goose-down comforter shifted and settled over his body.

Snow fluttered against the window. Alex listened to the wind whistle around the house, chasing itself and the snow.

Clara! Old Clara!

He was dressed and out of bed and downstairs almost in one movement. His hands were shaking so badly when he tried to lock the metal buckles of his galoshes that he had to stop and concentrate. Metal fitted into metal, flipped over, locked.

There was no wind at the moment, very little snow falling, but the snow that had fallen over the past few days had thickened the silence of the town, of the houses, and as he ran now his breaths and the rasp of his sleeves and trousers as they brushed cloth against cloth were the only sounds he could hear.

At Rosie's house he climbed the steps two at a time, slipped once, caught at the railing, righted himself, and continued. Inside, dangerously near the barely warm coal stove, was the wheelchair, empty. In the bedroom, Old Clara's red nose rose above her blankets like a landmark. Flat on her back in the bed, her arms and legs tied at the wrists and the ankles to the bedposts, the old woman seemed surprisingly alert, not exhausted at all. "Those men are gone. Call the cops.

Hurry, call the cops, Oliver. Call Sheriff Barnhardt. Hurry, hurry."

"I'm not Oliver, Clara, I'm Alex. I'll get you some food."

"I don't want food. I want these things cut. I want to get up. Call Sheriff Barnhardt."

He could not remind her that Sheriff Barnhardt had been dead for several years.

"No, no. Hepplewhite's the sheriff. Call Bobby Hepplewhite."

Bobby Hepplewhite had been chased out of office two years ago.

"We can't call the cops, Clara. The Germans have Rosie with them. If they come back and the cops are here, Dieter will kill Rosie." Alex was in the kitchen now, opening drawers, looking for a pair of scissors, but he had no luck. Giving up on the scissors, he used a carving knife.

As he cut at the bindings, she kept watching his face, seeming to move in and out of recognition. At one moment, her eyes shone bright and clear, and it seemed she was in better spirits than she had been in years. Then they clouded over, letting the thin, blue-veined eyelids almost close completely. Had they given her some kind of sleeping pill?

Once she was freed she kept rubbing her wrists against each other, as well as her ankles. She smelled as if she'd dirtied herself. Alex knew that before he left her he'd have to change her diaper, but the task was so awful that he put it out of his mind, hoping his interpretation of the smell would be proven wrong.

"Are you warm enough, Clara?"

She continued studying the ceiling and rubbing her wrists and ankles.

Once, in the kitchen, as he was putting cereal in a bowl for her, Alex heard her call his name. He went back to the bed. She was subdued but rational. Her voice was firm. She did not gag between words, between sentences. "You better take a look upstairs, Alex. Something going on up there. They talk German. I can hear them down here." She rolled her eyes a bit, fell asleep for a minute, opened her eyes, glanced about the room. Her eyes glazed over and cleared. "A man came here. Two times. A banker maybe. Wore a suit. Black suit."

After he helped Clara from the bed and into her wheelchair, Alex covered her with two blankets. No, he was not wrong about the diaper. Maybe he could just ignore it, pretend he hadn't noticed it, let Rosie deal with it when she returned this evening. A few hours wouldn't matter to Clara, who accepted her food now without much interest. She rambled on as if this was a normal morning while she ate her cereal. She said something about Oliver and about the prices at the store.

"He came yesterday," she said. "This time in uniform. Navy uniform. Went upstairs. Spoke German, English too. Good English. College professor. Funny things going on." Then she dropped her head and slept for about twenty seconds. When she awakened Alex told her he'd have to take her to the bed again, and tie her, as the Germans had. Otherwise they might be angry. And they didn't want to make those guys mad, did they? She did not resist at all. After he tied her wrists and ankles, with looser knots, he left her. She called after him, "Now you be careful over there, Oliver. Those Huns are not human. I know. You ask my husband. He'll tell you stories about the first war that'll curl your stomach. I mean your hair." That had obviously struck her as very funny, because she giggled for at least a minute, repeating "curl your stomach" twice.

Alex stood at the bottom of the six steps that led to the upstairs room, wondering if they could have left a trap for him. He'd read about clever traps that killed pursuers in France and Italy. Some actor in a recent movie about the combat that followed the D day landings had

91

stepped inch by inch through a deserted house. He'd tripped over a wire that triggered an explosion that killed him. Alex knelt and looked up across the steps. Sure enough! Halfway up a fine thread spanned the step's width. The same color as the wood, it could not be easily seen from above. Both ends had been glued to the walls. He would have gone up and down without knowing he'd broken it. The Germans would have known he'd been upstairs searching the room. He continued up the stairs, carefully avoiding the trap.

Sheets and blankets on a single bed were neatly, firmly tucked in. A badly upholstered chair waited before a long, narrow, dark table. The cellophane wrapper on the shade of the fake brass floor lamp was still intact. Alex went to the window. This was where that face had hovered the other evening. Down below, at the gate, was the iron drum. Now, when the men were gone, was the time to get that wallet.

But first things first. He had to find out what Old Clara was talking about. Or was she simply hallucinating?

Against the white wall stood a three-drawer dresser, with a framed oval mirror fixed to the top. On the dresser, under a clean, white towel, lay the violin that had belonged to Rosie's father, the bow alongside, also covered with a white towel.

The top drawer of the dresser contained four pairs of men's socks, each pair rolled into a tight ball. In the next drawer were men's underwear, shorts and undershirts, each neatly folded, and white handkerchiefs, probably a dozen, also neatly folded. In the bottom drawer were two stacks of white shirts. In the closet, on one hanger, two dark ties. On four separate hangers were four dresses. Two coats, women's coats. Two pairs of women's shoes. The shoes rested on a package of tissue.

Alex lifted the shoes. The tissue was wrapped around a package. Inside: radio tubes, pieces of metal, wires. He replaced everything as it had been. On rising he noticed a rope hanging behind the coats. He pushed the coats aside, disclosing a metal box. The metal hasp was closed with a sturdy lock. He made sure everything was as it had been when he'd begun his search.

He avoided the thread on his way down and approached Old Clara, wondering how much she knew. But she was snoring lightly, a serene smile on her lips. Before he left the house he replenished the fire.

Alex paused at the iron drum. He had the time and freedom now to work on the ice cover.

He dug down in the snow and found the screwdriver. After he wiped it clean, he bailed the snow out of the drum with his hands. Once he reached the ice, he went to work, striking with the screwdriver, lifting at the edges, striking and lifting, again and again. After he broke through, he upended the barrel. The water ran out, bringing with it a sludge of mud as well as paper and pieces of wood and flashlight batteries and chunks of tools forever rusted into one piece.

When there was no more water, he looked into the barrel. It was empty. Completely empty. There was no wallet. No penknife.

At two o'clock Alex returned to the Kilroy house to find Old Clara as he'd left her. She pleaded with him to untie her. "I have to go to the bathroom. You better let me go or you'll be sorry."

The diaper Rosie had fitted onto her was no longer performing its job. The odor in the room was almost too much, but Alex forced himself to go near the bed. He untied the wrist and ankle wraps and helped Clara stand. She and the bed linen formed one foul mess.

He led her into the bathroom and left her sitting there, wrapped in one of her blankets. Then, back at the bed, he pulled off the sheets, wiped the rubber pad, and dropped the soiled linen in a corner. He found clean linen on a shelf in a closet. While remaking the bed as best he could, he felt a chill on his back. The front door was open, and cold wind, as well as snow, were pouring in. Old Clara, wearing nothing but her soiled nightgown, was balancing her bony body against the push of the wind.

Alex brought her inside and gave her a steaming washcloth and a dry towel. He looked away while she obediently dabbed at her body with the washcloth. Then, determined not to let her return in that shape to the now clean bed, he took the cloth from her hand and cleaned her himself, using hot water and soap and then the towel. She did not complain or resist when he returned her to the bed and retied the wraps.

Alex stopped at Larry's house to ask him to come along on the paper route, but Larry was still angry. "You gonna tell me what you were gonna tell me?"

"I can't, Larry."

"Then do your route yourself. We have a radio now." He closed the door, but Alex had had time to see a large, tinsel-covered Christmas tree behind Larry. When Alex looked back, Larry was not at the window.

After he fitted the papers into the canvas bag, Alex walked along Main Street. He stopped in Critchlow's General Store to buy a Butterfinger bar for himself and a large mint wafer for Old Clara. Then, moving toward the café, he watched the crowd of soldiers and sailors boarding the bus for Boston. Maybe he could just get on a bus and ride somewhere, get off, be forgotten. Whatever might happen would not involve him. Later, in a week or two, he'd return. By then the whole affair might be over.

He shrugged his fantasy away, continued on past Steinhauser's Shoes for Men and the Gulf station, and entered the Pequod Café.

There were only three people at the counter and an elderly couple at a table. The Christmas tree blinked and sparkled, and a children's chorus was singing "Silent Night" on the radio. Alex sat on a stool at the counter and let the bag settle onto the floor. Lucy took both of his hands into her own. "Nothing new," she said. He nodded, and Lucy lifted his hands to kiss them. "Did you get some sleep, kiddo?" She reached out and felt his forehead. "You feel OK."

"I'm fine. I slept all morning."

He could see the back of her hair and her neck in the mirror. She looked into his eyes. "You worried, honey?"

"I'm fine."

She was looking into his eyes. "Larry was in. He asked if you were sick. You act like you're sick, he said."

He lifted the canvas bag onto his shoulder.

"Alex, is something—you know, not just Oliver— something else, is something wrong?"

He pretended it was necessary to count the newspapers, but Lucy was not impressed. She'd been the sister of paperboys too long. "What is it, sweetie?"

He wanted so much to tell her. She would help. She'd know what to do. She'd get Tony, and Tony would go to Chief Burnham. He took the easy way out by lying, feeling cheap at exploiting everyone's belief that it was only Oliver's fate that worried him, that drew those heavy circles under his eyes, that caused him to break into tears so easily. "I wish the war was over," he said. "I wish Oliver was home. The Tompkinses got one of those telegrams. The one Mom was talking about. Duane Tompkins. He was eighteen. Four years older than I am. Not even four."

Lucy tried to talk but turned away and used a counter cloth to wipe the exterior of the coffee urn. Then she turned. "We have to live our lives," she said. "I have to work at the café. Mom and Dad have to work at Electric Boat. You have to go to school. You have to study and get good grades. If Oliver wants anything he wants you to work hard at school and get good grades."

Lucy smiled a bit, pretending to be more content, he knew, than she really was. Was she happy, he wondered, being with Tony? Peg Leg Tony, some people called him. She'd hit a sailor with a heavy iron skillet last fall, after the sailor had said she'd be happier with him than she could ever be with that peg leg. The sailor was on the floor, a large lump on his forehead, before Tony could get out of the kitchen.

He might be able to tell her everything if it was all happening to one of his friends. But she would tell Tony, and his temper would drive him to the house and through the door and . . . and they'd shoot Rosie and Old Clara and probably Tony as well.

Lucy walked him to the door. "He won't be killed, Alex."

"How do you know?"

"I know."

Her certainty was contagious. He left the café feeling much better and waving back as she called that she'd see him at supper. He could have all the mince pie he could eat.

He went back to the General Store to buy another candy bar. How could he bring candy just for Old Clara? Rosie deserved a bar, too. Her favorite was Power House, even if it did threaten to pull out her false teeth.

As he passed the bus station on the way to his first customer, the Greyhound (from Boston) was unloading several servicemen, including two WACs. Larry called the women soldiers Whackos.

He almost called out when Rosie appeared behind the WACs, pausing on the top step. Two elderly women behind her were chirping like fat sparrows, informing everyone within hearing that they were so pleased finally to be in Pequod, Connecticut. They pronounced it, in chorus, "Co-nec-ti-cut."

Alex watched the courteous bus driver deposit the ladies' luggage (suitcases, cardboard boxes, bulging paper bags) near the entry to the General Store. He heard Joe Critchlow welcome Rosie, who introduced the two women as her aunts. He then welcomed the ladies to Pequod and urged them to have a happy holiday. How long would they be staying?

"A month," the shorter of the two women said, "if we don't drive Miss Rose and her dear mother crazy before that."

Rosie asked Joe Critchlow if someone in the store could drive her and her aunts home if she did some shopping. He promised to find someone. He might even drive them himself.

The shorter woman bounced over to Alex, whose mouth remained wide open. She reached out and, with the fingers of her right hand, gently closed the boy's mouth. "And what is your name, little boy?"

"M-m-my name is Alex."

"Oh dear," she said, depositing a pat on the top of his head, "you must master that stammer."

Alex climbed the steps of the Kilroy house, hearing the laughter inside even before Rosie opened the door for him. The two women sat at the table, their faces flushed from the warmth or, perhaps, from what they considered a fine practical joke performed at the expense of Americans. Even the usually grim face of Dieter held a smile at Alex's entry.

Old Clara, wrapped in blankets in her wheelchair, sat in front of the stove, leaning forward slightly to catch whatever extra heat might be available. Rosie danced about in her welcome, as if success or return had more than compensated for her terrors of the early morning. She tried to get her mother to recognize Alex's presence, but the old woman, her face blank, stared at the stove's door as if she were trying to will it open.

Suitcases and boxes, all but one still closed, were scattered about the room. In spite of his anger, Alex could not deny his relief, even pleasure, that all had apparently gone well. Anything to ease the chance of anger or frustration excusing abuse of Rosie or her mother.

Dieter, sauntering over to the one open box, closed the flaps.

Hans raised his cup of steaming coffee. "Well, Herr Alex? Do we receive rewards for our theater?"

"You sure bought a lot of stuff."

Hans waved Alex's curiosity aside. "Gifts for when we return. And Miss Rose? She had an elegant lunch. A gift from her two old-maid aunts. Do you say *aunts* or *aunties*? Everyone in Pequod knows she has guests, two aunts from New York. No one will be suspicious when we travel now."

Dieter laughed, then emptied a bottle of beer in one long swallow. "Too easy," Dieter said. He could not keep his goodwill alive more than a minute or two. He waved a long, slim hand at the American world outside the house. "Like taking candy from a baby. I almost wish there were more challenges. You Americans. So gullible."

"What's *gullible* mean?"

Hans, enjoying the opportunity to be the teacher, said, "Easily fooled."

"Where did you learn English?" Alex asked. "You don't have any accent at all. And you know bigger words than I do. Both of you."

Hans, grinning impishly, waved a finger at Alex, as if alert to his tricks. He left the table to go to one of the suitcases. Rustling about in the paper inside, he withdrew two long, flat boxes, one of which he opened. Inside were eight fine carving knives and a sharpening stone. "Look at this, Alex. Very special tools. And look." From the same box he brought out a block of wood about the size of his fist. "Pine. Perfect. Come, bring your cocoa over here. Sit. Closer, closer, I won't bite you. This"—and he gave a second box to Alex—"is for you."

98

Inside were a duplicate set of knives and a sharpening stone. "A block of wood for you. You are about to get your first carving lesson."

Alex wasn't certain about his reaction. He should not stay any longer, and he certainly should not stay and play with these men. But the offer of the gift had surprised him.

"Merry Christmas," Hans said, and he selected a knife. Alex lifted out the corresponding knife from his own box. Hans settled the block between thumb and forefinger of his left hand and pared away a thin crescent of wood. Alex did the same. For the next half hour, using four different knives, Alex removed thin shavings of pine. Suddenly he saw a face beginning to emerge from the block. He worked on, ignoring time, ignoring his cocoa and his cookies, ignoring Old Clara's snores, Rosie's sighs and yawns, Dieter's growing impatience for . . . for what? For Hans to stop this foolishness? After he spoke a rapid, curt German word, Hans nodded and said, "Three more minutes."

Hans took the block Alex had been cutting. "My, my, look at that. An elephant."

Alex laughed. "It's not an elephant. It's a dog."

"Of course. My mistake. Ach, how could I be so blind?"

Alex laughed, then caught himself.

"There," Hans said.

In the palm of the German saboteur's hand was the face and head of Alex. A strong, true image. Alex wanted to say thanks, but the word refused to come. He grabbed the head and ran home through the snow.

9

The letter must have been mailed in early December. Long before the German breakthrough at Ardennes. The now threatening Battle of the Bulge.

Hey little brother,

Yesterday here at the rest camp we got our mail that was backed up for weeks. Both your letters sent right before Thanksgiving came in the same mail call. Along with letters from Lucy and Mom and Dad. Even had 1 from Tony, and he's probably not written more than 3 letters his whole life. I wish I was there for Thanksgiving supper.

Hope this war ends before you get to 18, Alex. Everywhere you look over here you see Nazis. Captured Nazis, wounded Nazis, dead Nazis. But you talk to the people, no one's ever been a Nazi. The elite guys called the SS, they're the worst.

Been thinking lots about Mom and Dad. Pretty soon Dad's going to be too old to be crawling round on greasy decks in storms wet and cold, 10,12 hours a day, 5 days a week. Ain't Mom something? Sent me a picture of her in I think a sub, her welder's mask up, her face all dirty, patched overalls. I remember she changed dresses 3 times a day.

Luce, she's got a good man. Me and Tony known each other all my life. You and me we're gonna have to take care of Mom and Dad when they get older. Maybe we'll get a bigger boat.

Fishing's all I know but maybe you'll go to college, be a doctor or lawyer or someone doesn't have to work so hard. I'll tell you. If I try real hard I can smell herring on my hands. Like it's in my skin, in my blood even. I get homesick. OK little brother study hard. Love, Oliver.

The fifth or sixth time Alex read the letter, he had such an intense need for Oliver in this room that he walked from wall to wall, touched each piece of clothing hanging in the closet, as if the feel, the scent, of the cloth, might bring his brother's body back.

"I brought some pictures of my brother. I want to carve him. Do you think I can?"

"Let's see the pictures, Alex."

When, in his room, bending over Oliver's desk, Alex had picked through the photographs, he'd called back his brother's voice, called back the feel of his clothes, called back his jokes about the fishing inadequacies of various friends. He'd filtered out every memory of Oliver being angry or vengeful or impatient. There was only the kind Oliver: delivering groceries to the Kilroys, digging their tiny plot of rocky earth, planting and watering and weeding the meager patch of tomatoes and flowers.

What would Oliver think when he received those copies of the *Courier-Journal* that had the photographs of him and Larry and the story of the saboteurs? Would he be as proud of Alex as Alex was of him? And what would he think when he eventually learned the truth?

Now, watching the fingers of the German, Hans, sorting the pictures, spreading them out, rearranging them, Alex wanted to scoop them up and deny his request to sculpt the figure of Oliver. Just lying there on the table in the presence of the spy, being considered, evaluated, by the German spy, they were sure to be soiled from now on. There was a bit of indecency, mockery perhaps, in the short, stocky man's still wearing women's clothing. In his stocking feet, the belt forgotten, the shapeless dress made him look like a somewhat crazy clown.

Dieter, who looked absolutely evil in his dress, his long, bony bare feet so white, came to peer over Hans's shoulder. "One Hundred First Airborne Division." The contempt in his voice was about to find its way into a nasty comment. Before it had time to develop Alex reached for the pictures, but Hans caught his hand. "Please leave them, Alex. We must study them." Hans spoke to Dieter in German, and spoke softly. Dieter paled; his body stiffened and his shoulders drew back. He all but saluted. Hans spoke again, again quietly, again in German. Dieter's head snapped; he whirled and went into the kitchen, where he poured coffee into a large mug and sipped the liquid as if it offered nourishment. Then he suddenly set the mug on the sink board and marched into the living room, where he selected two of the cardboard boxes brought from New London. He stomped up the stairs.

Rosie came out of her mother's bedroom. "What's wrong? Is something wrong?"

Hans shook his head. "Go back to your mother, Miss Rose."

Exhausted from the day's journey, and probably at the end of her patience with her own inability to improve matters, Rosie looked as old as her mother.

"Please close the door behind you," Hans said.

Head bowed, her slippers scraping the floor, Rosie returned to her mother's room and obediently closed the door.

Hans shifted the pictures on the table, muttering, cocking his head, covering a portion of one picture with his hand, then a portion of another. "Good wide forehead," he said. "A strong chin. We work from these three pictures. It will take an hour. Perhaps two."

"I better go. I should be home."

Hans pushed his chair back. "Stay, please. We will work fast. But first I must speak to Dieter."

Alex watched the German's body disappear as he climbed the stairs to the attic. He was still wearing hose, so the last of him to disappear from view was the heavy, brown feet. When he came back down, he was in better spirits. He smiled as he selected one of the three pictures. Oliver, in a white T-shirt, fatigue pants, and jump boots, was sitting on the steps of his barracks. "Your brother is what here? Twenty? Twenty-one?"

"Nineteen. No, eighteen."

Hans's mouth thinned, tightened, and the muscles at the corners of his jaws quivered. He turned the photograph over and labored over the scrawl. "Fort Benning, Georgia. May, 1943. Me after my first jump. The worst is over." His eyes still on the photograph, Hans permitted himself a slight grunt. "The worst is still to come, my young comrade."

Comrade? Alex thought he hadn't heard correctly. Comrade? This ugly woman-man, this spy, identifying Oliver as his comrade? Was he trying to be funny?

Hans leaned back and shrugged. "Comrade-in-arms. In battle. The same battle, different armies. Fifty years from now we both will tell stories to our grandchildren. We will speak different languages about the same war. If Odysseus and Achilles and Hector lived they would have told their grandchildren stories like we tell our grandchildren. They were comrades-in-arms." He stopped, sensing, apparently, the confusion in Alex's mind. "Do you not know who Odysseus was? Or Achilles or Hector? Do you know about the Trojan War?"

"No."

Hans laughed and slapped his forehead. "I cannot stop being the professor. A . . . hmm . . . a pedant. Do you know what a pedant is?"

"No."

"A pedant is someone who can't help trying to

teach someone something. He thinks he knows everything. A pedant is a . . . a bore. I promise not to bore
you again." He rested his chin in his right hand and
winked at Alex. "You are proud of your brother."

"Sure I'm proud of him. I wish—"

"No, don't say it."

"Say what? What was I going to say?"

"You wish you could be in the army. You wish you
could be fighting also."

"I was thinking that."

Hans reached down to a box beneath the table and
brought up a block of pine about twice the size of his
fist. He turned it over and around, seeming to evaluate
the grain, the size, the shape, the color.

"What are you thinking?" Alex asked.

Hans leaned back and looked at him. He seemed at
ease, content. They might be old friends taking shelter
together from bad weather. They might have just come
in from a long walk or a movie. They were not, had
never been, enemies. Hans, like a dog just out of water,
shook his head, as if trying to rid himself of something
disturbing. "Come. We get to work. While you work I
play."

He went upstairs and came down, carrying the
violin and the bow.

Hans set out the knives. After cutting away the corners
of the block of wood, he shaped the piece into a large
egg on a stem. With a finer blade he removed thinner
slabs, leaving flat planes that approximated the planes
of Oliver's cheeks and temple and forehead. "Now you
take it, Alex. Use the knife like a pencil. You should
begin here, with the forehead. A good place to start.
See how broad Oliver's forehead is. From the top of the
nose, where the eyebrows meet, the forehead slopes
back just so. Skim away this part here, carefully, trying
to catch that slope."

Alex worked slowly, carefully, glancing at the photographs between strokes for guidance.

"Trust your memory, too, Alex. You know him better than the photographs do."

Hans lifted the violin and tucked it up under his chin. He swayed slightly as he played. Quietly at first, then a bit louder, stronger. Alex forgot his vision of the comic, this stocky man in a dress forgetting now, in this room, all need to pretend feminine mannerisms. Hans stopped playing, advised Alex, played more, advised. He took the wood to show where a blade stroke by a certain knife might bring out a shape or, occasionally, he recut to correct a swell or depression.

Rosie very quietly opened the door so she and her mother could hear the music. Hans, eyes closed, either was unaware or didn't care.

"Do you know Haydn, Alex?"

Alex said no.

"Wait. Rest a moment. I will play his *Emperor* Quartet. I hope you remember the names. Haydn. *Emperor* Quartet. My son plays it on the cello. We play it together sometimes. His mother plays the viola." Hans tested a few notes, tightened a string, tested again, tightened again. He stopped, waved the bow at Alex, said, "Haydn, *Emperor* Quartet," and laughed. "Officially," he said, "it is the String Quartet in C Major, Opus 76. Quartet. Four players. I am only one." He began again and played for several minutes.

Rosie, in the doorway, had obviously forgiven Hans and Dieter any discourtesy or pain they'd brought into this house. The music was more than compensation; it was heavenly. She was smiling, as was Alex, not so much smiling as letting himself bathe in the glow of the music. When Hans stopped his eyes remained closed for a moment, then he withdrew the instrument from beneath his chin and set the violin and the bow on the table. He covered both with the towel.

"I heard you playing that the other night."

"You did? You were outside listening?"

"It is the most beautiful music I've ever heard."

Dieter, upstairs, shouted down the stairway, "It is *Deutschland über alles!*" And he sang in a loud, not very musical voice, *"Deutschland, Deutschland, über alles, über . . ."*

"Enough," Hans called.

". . . über alles und der Welt. Deutsch—"

Hans shouted in German. It was without doubt an order.

Dieter's voice died away.

"What's that mean?" Alex asked.

"It means Germany, Germany, over all . . . over the whole world. Haydn composed long before the Nazis appeared in Germany. The tune became our anthem. He did not write the words."

Upstairs Dieter's coarse voice was approximating the tune. Over and over.

They worked for nearly an hour, with Hans hovering close, ready to caution, to guide, to take Alex's hand in his own to demonstrate the angle the blade might be held for this or that kind of cut. "Here. The nostrils, the cleft in the upper lip beneath the nose. Much of the impression our face makes is decided here. See how Oliver's lip curves up? No one who knows Oliver has ever put into words this place here, this nose-lip-chin space, but this is what decides Oliver's face. Maybe, a bit, the distance between the eyes. Much wider than mine. Like yours."

"I never noticed that before."

"You noticed without knowing you noticed."

"His eyes are like my mother's. It's the upper lids."

"Very good, very good. In English it is called hooded. The upper lid comes down over the orb farther than on most people. You have such eyes."

"Where'd you learn all this, Hans?"

"After *Gymnasium*, what you call high school, I

came to visit relatives in Pittsburgh. The state of Pennsylvania. I studied art and English. Carnegie Tech University. My mother wanted I should—excuse me—wanted me to become a sculptor, so I became a history teacher. A pedant." He pushed back his chair. "Shall we have cocoa?"

"It's getting late. We're having a big supper at the café. Mom and Dad aren't working tonight."

"Miss Rose tells me they work at Electric Boat. They help construct submarines."

Alex wasn't quite sure why he felt he shouldn't comment on that, but he didn't.

"Fifteen minutes' work will finish your sculpture. I'll be back."

Hans climbed the stairs with a youthful bounce, his dress swirling. Dieter came down twice, his big, ugly, white feet like pieces of lifeless, hard marble, to return each time with one of the boxes. Alex might as well not have been there. Upstairs the two men spoke in German. The volume of a radio went up, loudly, then decreased to silence. Hans came down. At the stove he made a cup of cocoa for Alex and one for himself.

After tossing two large chunks of coal into the stove and washing his hands, Hans returned to the table. His right hand went to his shirt pocket and came out with a white card. With two white cards. The edge of his hand cleared the table in front of him, letting the shavings fall into his lap. His sleeve polished the table, and he set the cards there, handling them as if they might shatter if they were treated too roughly. "The one rule I disobeyed." He touched one card, then the other, saying, in turn, "Günther, Helga Maria." He thought for a moment. "Günther is your age."

"Do you miss them?"

Hans nodded. "Love is not pneumonia or consumption, but it can sometimes be fatal."

"What was the rule you disobeyed?"

"Never never *never* carry on your person documents

that might compromise you, that might be used to identify you."

"How could these photographs identify you?"

"Do they look like German children?"

"They look like lots of children in Pequod."

"Turn them over."

On the back a small red circle contained the words *Troy, New York*. Blue words had been stamped above the circle: *Russel's Drugs*.

"Forged," Hans said. "I had to have them with me. But the pictures had to make police—if they caught me—think they were American children."

"Is there a Russel's Drugs in Troy, New York?"

"Of course."

"Where were they taken?"

"In a park near Salzburg. Austria. Do their clothes look foreign?"

"No, they look American. Why are you so scared? You're really in charge. You make the rules, don't you?"

"I'm in charge? Of what?"

"Of the whole thing, the whole spy thing. Dieter knows you're the boss. He might not like it but he knows it."

"His antagonism is a problem; it is too obvious."

"Sometimes it looks like he's a private and you're a captain."

Hans picked up the two photographs—two precious jewels—and tucked them into his shirt pocket. "Not too far from the truth." He reached over to guide Alex's hand, then took the sculpture and peeled the thinnest of shavings, almost dust, from the body of the nose. He gave the piece back to Alex and watched him continue the shaping. "You are precocious," he said. "Your second carving, and it's very good. My second was not nearly so good." When Alex refused to acknowledge the flattery, Hans said, "Can you try not to be angry with me?" He smiled wistfully. "But of course you're angry. Why shouldn't you be? Tell me. These children in my

108

pictures. Do you think their father could kill an American boy if the boy threatened our mission?"

"We're at war."

"War makes such things so different?"

"Doesn't it? You're the grown-up, grown-ups decided there had to be a war. Kids don't decide those things."

"I do not think so. Your brother, Oliver. I'm sure he's a good man. Could he kill a German child?"

"I bet he wouldn't."

"You sound uncertain. Are you?"

"Well, if the child had a gun and was going to kill him, yeah, maybe then."

Hans stared into space, probably wondering if there was any reason to continue this exchange. "We are almost finished," he said.

Hans took the finished piece and held it at arm's length. He could not admire it enough. He just kept nodding his head and turning the piece and nodding. When Hans, the stocky woman who had to be an officer in the German army, held the door open, Alex waited, dawdling over zippers and buckles and buttons.

"Do you remember who composed the music I played, Alex?"

"Haydn."

"The name of the music?"

"*Emperor* Quartet."

"Very good. You get an A."

The night air burned Alex's nostrils as he breathed. He tried to run, but his galoshes were too heavy. When he finally reached his porch, the snow on the wooden steps crackled under his feet. Inside, on the radio, a chorus was singing "O Little Town of Bethlehem."

His father opened the door. "Thought I heard you out here. You comin' in?"

Alex removed his galoshes, slapped them free of

snow, and stepped inside. He hung his cap and jacket on the rack. His mother asked where he'd been. Tony had gone to Larry's house to track him down, but he wasn't there. Did he remember they were all going to the café for dinner? Hadn't he said he was going to Larry's house? They were not trying to trap him, they were concerned about him, trying to demonstrate that concern.

Alex went to his jacket and returned with his hands behind his back. "I have a Christmas present. It's two days late. And it's not wrapped. But it's for everyone. OK?"

Nods, agreement, permission.

Alex held out his hands, raising both palms so the sculpture could be seen by him as well.

His mother moved her face so close her eyelashes could almost flick the wooden cheek of Oliver's face. His father, rising from the sofa and almost stumbling as he climbed over his wife's outstretched legs, asked three times, "Did you carve this?" He took the sculpture in his hands, held it, then offered it to Alex's mother. She stood and took a few paces to the left, to see it in better light; then, with great care, she lifted it to the mantel above the fireplace. "Did you carve it, Alex?"

"I had some help, but I did it."

His father, usually laconic, usually unable or unwilling to demonstrate affection, put an arm around his wife's shoulders. He kept shaking his head, as if he, who did not believe in miracles, had just witnessed a miracle.

"I never knew you were an artist," his mother said.

"I did have some help. A little."

"From whom, for goodness' sake?"

"Mr. Tollefson, your art teacher?" his father said.

Alex was about to confess that yes, it had been Mr. Tollefson, when his mother ran from the room. His father put an arm around his shoulders, drew him close. "You'll know sooner or later," he said. "The War

110

Department's just about given up hope for the Hundred First Airborne Division. They've taken heavy casualties. They're out of medical supplies. General Patton's relief force is close, but it's being slowed down by German panzers." He glanced at the wall map. Alex could not look.

"I think we still ought to go to that supper. It'll help distract us, Alex."

At the mantel, Alex wished he might be able to wipe the wood clean of every touch of Hans's fingers. Had Hans known, while he'd been helping Alex, that the 101st—no, not just the 101st but Oliver—had he known that both were possibly doomed? He must have. They had that old radio. Dieter had been upstairs. Hans had gone up several times. They'd spoken German.

Alex reached over to the hooded eyes. If he could only close them completely, so they wouldn't be staring at him.

10

Three days after Christmas.

At the sound of the knock Alex went to the door, knowing it had to be Larry. It was.

Larry stood there, beaming, his new plaid mackinaw like a small tent.

"Wanted to show you my new mackinaw. What'd you get, Alex?"

"Oh, I got a wristwatch and some clothes and some books. Stuff like that."

"First new mackinaw I've ever gotten. I've always worn my brothers' jackets when they got too tight for them. Can I come in? It's cold out here."

"Sure. Come in."

Alex automatically loaded a plateful of leftover casserole for Larry, even though he insisted he'd already had lunch. "Nice mackinaw," Alex said.

"Yeah. I got hightop shoes too. Got them before Christmas, though. Mom and Dad got jobs at Electric Boat."

Alex said he was glad. What shift were they working? Larry said they started tomorrow at eight o'clock.

"We're gonna get a phone. It takes a month, but we're gonna get it."

The lunch dragged on. After the pie Alex took Larry upstairs, to talk, but all Alex wanted to do was to listen to the news on the radio. For a few minutes Larry seemed to be interested.

The Germans were continuing to advance. The Allied forces seemed disorganized, almost in panic. The worst thing was the weather. The Allied air forces could not give the slightest aid to the ground forces. Names and designations of fighting units were withheld, as were the number and names of killed and wounded.

"Pretty weird Christmas," Larry said. He'd already lost interest in the radio news and wandered to the desk, where he surveyed the photographs of Oliver and then the books on the shelves. "Sixteen . . . seventeen . . . eighteen books. You read all these?"

"Most of them. Oh, all of them, I guess."

"No wonder you do better than I do in school. You read all these books."

Alex knew Larry wasn't here to count books. He was so transparent. He'd come over to renew the friendship but was too proud to admit it. OK, Alex wouldn't make him beg. In fact, he was so glad that Larry was here he considered going back on his refusal to tell Larry about the two Germans.

"Pap said your brother Oliver's at Bas . . . whatever that place is in the war."

"Bastogne."

"Yeah, Bastogne."

"It doesn't look good, Larry. Oliver's been lucky so far. He's been wounded once. He's a sergeant now. Sergeants get killed more than lieutenants or captains."

"You heard about—"

"Yeah, I heard. Two telegrams from the War Department to Pequod. Wait. Listen."

113

*It is vital that Bastogne be held. There, where the Liège-
Arlon highway meets six other roads, two miles out of town,
paratroopers from the One Hundred First Division have set
up a line of foxholes. Between the foxholes and the town is
the final-effort defense circle, manned mainly by strag-
glers. The acting commander of the One Hundred First—
slight but sassy General Anthony Clement McAuliffe—calls
the inner line his "Team Snafu." Behind Team Snafu, inside
the town, a force of tanks and tank destroyers are held in
reserve, ready to rush out against a major enemy attack.
General McAuliffe calls these men and their machines his
Fire Brigade. On the first night in Bastogne the besieged One
Hundred First suffered the worst fate possible: its complete
surgical unit was captured by the Germans. That means that
wounded soldiers cannot have amputations, cannot even rely
on splints to hold fractured bones, cannot appeal to skilled
medical teams.*

Alex turned off the radio. "I have to get out of
here."

"Sure. Let's go to my house."

"Sure, Larry, anywhere." He rushed from the
room.

Eliza, Larry's youngest sister, opened the door before
they reached the porch. She'd been watching their
approach through the window. "See my Christmas
gift?" she said, holding her new doll aloft.

Larry's brother Byron, who was sixteen, was wearing his new high-tops and his new jacket.

Alex laughed. "You wear your jacket in the house?"

Byron had to demonstrate the depth of the pockets,
the promised warmth of the hood, and the zipper that
was guaranteed never to fail. "Mom, Dad, it's Alex
Kellar. Did you give Alex his present, Larry?"

114

Larry pushed Byron. "You ruined everything. I was gonna surprise him."

Byron snickered. "Forget it, Alex. Larry doesn't have a gift for you. He gave it to me."

"I do so," Larry countered.

Alex said, "That's not fair. I didn't get you a present. We've never given gifts to each other."

Larry leaned close. "You gave me the best gift ever. That money. Look."

The entire Cobb family was sprawled around the living room, which still smelled not just of pine but of gingerbread. Eliza lifted one of the cookies from a bough of the tree and offered it to Alex. Everyone seemed to be smiling or laughing or offering Alex a cup of cider or chocolates from a fancy box bought at Critchlow's General Store.

The girls clamored for attention, begging him to appreciate their new phonograph armed with the record of Bing Crosby singing "White Christmas" over and over and over. "White Christmas" appeared to be the only record in the house. Mr. Cobb, who had shaved and had his famous long, unruly hair trimmed to almost fashionable length, was wearing a white shirt. He looked so respectable he could have walked into the General Store and been considered the new town lawyer or doctor. He even treated his wife with a new civility, going into the kitchen to check on her while she was preparing dinner. Mrs. Cobb was studying a new Sears, Roebuck catalog. "Now that I'm a workin' gal," she explained, "I've got to get me things." She reeled off a variety of items: gear for the boat, tools, clothes for the girls and Larry, some new dresses for Amelia, who'd also be working.

"Amelia? Is she working at Electric Boat too?"

"Didn't Lawrence tell you? That picture of Lawrence in the newspaper was a passport into heaven. Me and Ellsworth got on at Electric Boat, and Amelia's gonna work at the post exchange on the base. In the kitchen. A cook. She gets wages and two meals a day. Amelia, you want a new pair of shoes? White, like nurse's shoes?"

"I'll see if they're required. Alex, you want to eat supper with us? Lawrence's had hundreds of meals at your house or the café. How 'bout it?"

"I wish I could, Amelia. But I better be heading back."

"Come on, Alex. I'm gonna eat." Larry punched him, a new demonstration of self-assurance, of the kind of camaraderie displayed on playgrounds.

"Well, I'll sit with you for a while."

The kids cheered. Larry went to the tree to paw among the miniature mountain of paper and tissue and ribbons and came up with a small package. "Merry Christmas, Alex."

Alex removed the red ribbon and tore the red paper from the little box. "A penknife. You remembered I lost mine."

"It's a Barlow. The best. It's got four blades. Pap sharpened it on his whetstone, so watch your fingers. It's like a razor."

"Show you something," Mr. Cobb said. He took the knife, opened the large blade, snapped a hair from his head, held out the hair, brought down the blade, and cut the hair in half. Larry, ebullient, asked if he could try the same trick, pulled a hair from his head. But he, unlike his father, cried out in pain and gave up. His father pulled a hair from his head again, extended his arm, and let Larry bring down the blade. It clipped the hair very close to his father's fingers. "Not quite so close the next time, Lawrence," his father said. "I need all my fingers for my new job."

The novelty of such humor and cheer in the house was as appealing as a new movie at the Majestic. Alex wasn't feeling just charitable toward Larry, or superior, the strong knight helping the poor, weak victim; he felt drawn to the new strength he saw in Larry. Larry would

116

not be the servile playmate at school now, accepting nasty comments from other kids. There was a promise of surprise. He even, to a slight degree, demonstrated his new assurance in exchanges with his father. "Pap, I bet I can cut a hair even closer to your finger." He wouldn't be given the opportunity, his father said. "Watch." Larry rose from the table, asked for Alex's knife, and swaggered toward his father. His mother shrieked, and his father, half scowling, half grinning, pointed a finger at his son, stopping him in his tracks. "Aw," Larry said, "you never let me have any fun." His sisters, as well as his mother, pounded the table and laughed and, in this new lenient atmosphere, howled their pleasure at both brother and father.

Alex sat through the meal without once thinking about Bastogne or the Battle of the Bulge or Oliver. When it was time for him to leave, he gestured with his head, and Larry, comprehending, followed him out of the house, only stopping at the door to zip his jacket and pull up and secure the hood. He tugged the draw-string too tightly. His face looked like a large red apple. He pretended to gag and loosened the string.

Outside, picking their way through the deep snow, the friends were silent for the first few minutes, savoring their new trust in each other. "I have to talk to you, Larry. I need help."

"Hey, forget it. You tricked me once already."

"This isn't a trick. I'm in a jam. You're the only one I can talk to. I need help."

"Well, you can trust me." Larry moved so close their arms brushed against each other. "What is it?"

"Can you come over to my house tomorrow night? There are still lots of leftovers."

Larry drew back, suspicious. "It's another trick. Why can't you tell me now?"

"I have to take you someplace, have to show you something. Until we can go there I can't tell you anything."

"Huh uh. You're playing tricks again. You aren't fair, Alex."

"I'm in a jam, a real jam. It's terrible. With Oliver over there, dying maybe, and me here with . . . with this. I don't know what to do, Larry."

"Hey, are you gonna cry? I never saw you cry about anything. You didn't even cry that time you broke your arm. Or that day Oliver got on the army train. Everyone else was bawlin', but you were old Alex Stoneface."

Alex thought at first that he'd stumbled, but his legs just gave out, just refused to keep him upright. He sat down in the snow.

"Hey, Alex, gee. It's . . . you bet I'll help. I'll do whatever you say. Come on, Alex, get up. It'll be OK. You wait and see."

Alex lifted his hand to knock, but Rosie swung the door open before his knuckles touched the wood.

The smell of roasted turkey and freshly baked bread swooped out of the kitchen. Hans stood at the stove, a white towel tied around his waist. Dieter, at the table, looking bored and put-upon, was setting napkins and silver. Old Clara, in her wheelchair in front of the coal stove, was chewing a slice of bread, her face smeared with jam. She was giggling as she ate, shaking her head. When the door had slammed closed and Alex had removed his galoshes and jacket, Old Clara brought up her head. She stared, straining to focus, and then, promptly alert, she winked at Alex.

Then she plopped the remainder of the bread into her mouth, giggled, turned her head, and stared at him as if he had just that moment appeared. "You home from the war, Oliver? You gonna take over the paper route? Your little brother's a nice boy, but he ain't you, Oliver."

Dieter grunted, looked through all the windows, grunted again. "Stupid, senile old witch."

118

Hans, stooped to baste the turkey in the oven, straightened. He spoke in his harsh, snapping German.

Dieter jerked his head, all but clicked his heels. "I apologize. Good evening to all of Germany's enemies." Hans, still annoyed, accepted the cynical apology.

Alex took the wet cloth from Old Clara's lap and wiped the jam from her face. She lifted her chin and turned just enough so no one else could see her kiss Alex lightly but firmly on his cheek.

When Alex insisted he could not stay, Hans did not press. Dieter wanted the parting on his terms, obviously, so he went upstairs and turned up the radio's volume, wanting the news of Germany's continuing conquest to be heard by all. Hans started to advise him to turn it down but paused. He too was now, suddenly, interested in the voice. It carried a rising note of buoyancy, a new tone of expectation.

This is H. K. Morrison reporting to you from London. If any action in this terrible war illustrates the contrast in character between the American and the German fighting forces, foot soldiers, and generals, it is the story of Bastogne. Just before the Germans charged out of the gloomy, blood-soaked Hürtgen Forest, Field Marshal Gerd von Rundstedt proclaimed to his troops: "Your great hour has struck. Strong attacking armies are advancing today . . . "

Dieter, downstairs again, had not yet sensed that change. The snide, self-satisfied snarl of a grin was still on his face.

". . . against the Anglo-Americans. I do not need to say more to you. You all feel it. Everything is at stake. You bear the holy duty to achieve the superhuman for our fatherland and our Führer."

That from General Gerd von Rundstedt. For five days it has seemed that the German troops were about to accom-

plish the superhuman for their fatherland and for their Führer. As the German advance continued, the holding of two positions grew enormously important to the Allies. One was the town of Malmedy, to the north of the German penetration, the other was the village of Bastogne to the south. The American unit charged with the holding of Bastogne was the One Hundred First Airborne Division, the Screaming Eagles. The Germans outnumbered the Americans four to one. After the first day, when the division's surgical unit was captured, American soldiers received no medical care. By the fourth day the town was littered with wounded and dead and dying American soldiers. Through the lines came a German envoy carrying, waving, a white flag. He delivered an ultimatum from General von Rundstedt: the Americans had two hours to surrender.

Even Old Clara was listening with a new intensity. There was no doubt at all that every word was clear. Hans and Dieter stood at the end of the table, their faces blank. Blank but pale. Alex felt a promise of change in the air, and he knew that they too were feeling it.

If they did not surrender, they would be annihilated by German artillery. General Anthony McAuliffe printed a one-word reply but delivered it with formal military courtesy: "To the German Commander—Nuts!—from the American Commander." To guarantee correct interpretation, an officer translated for the blindfolded German envoy. "It means the same as Go to Hell!" The Americans have continued to turn back every German attack. Now we hear the news that General Patton's forces are drawing closer and closer to Bastogne. There is a feeling swelling now throughout the Allied ranks that the German Wehrmacht will not succeed. Everything, indeed, as General von Rundstedt said, was at stake. The holy duty to achieve the superhuman for their fatherland and their Führer has failed. With the failure to take Bastogne, the Battle of the Bulge is all but over. The Germans have lost the war. This is a very proud American, H. K. Morrison, reporting to you from London.

Dieter waited for some reaction, perhaps for advice, from Hans. As if for the moment he did not trust his own senses. But Hans was no more prepared for the news than Dieter had been. When Hans remained silent, then dropped into a chair as if all the wind had just been knocked out of him, Dieter tossed the remaining napkins and silver on the table and climbed the stairs to the attic.

Hans's face was still very pale. "General von Rundstedt is one of our best. It was our last effort. Doomed, foolish perhaps, but it had to be tried." He shrugged. "We will fight on, of course. The war is over, but, unfortunately, it has not ended."

Dieter shouted from the attic. "Lies. All lies. Typical lies. The American press cannot admit defeat." Then he lapsed into German.

"In English, Dieter!"

"It is not over. We shall triumph!"

Hans went to the foot of the stairs. Did he want Alex to hear and understand, or did he feel the German language inappropriate for the confession? "You are beginning to bore me with your mindless arrogance and stupidity. But you will be pleased, I think, to know that I plan to continue our mission." He came to Alex. "Your brother. Have you heard news?"

"No."

"Perhaps he will survive. Many will."

"What did you mean? The mission continues."

"I am a German soldier. The war continues and, so, unfortunately, must I. I have not been relieved or discharged. I will not ignore orders."

"But if it's all over . . . can't you just surrender?"

"No. It is futile, of course, but we have our orders."

121

"It's crazy. You'll be killed."

Hans smiled. "Correct. But perhaps, in the process, you shall learn a bit about duty. Your brother teaches you, I teach you. I, the perpetual teacher. However, I am pleased you're concerned."

"I could go to the police."

"Do not do that, Alex. We—Dieter and I—are now quite desperate. We are still in this house, we still must continue our control of your two women. It is not chivalry, perhaps, but chivalry died two, no, three, centuries ago. It is war. Would your brother ever disobey an order? Of course not. That is one reason he is on the winning side. Now, friend Alex, you had best go. Perhaps we should say farewell. I wish facts were different. But facts are facts. You and my son should meet. Perhaps, someday, in the future . . . But go now."

The moon was brilliant silver, almost white. He could see clear to the coast. If he stopped crunching the snow beneath his feet, he could hear the tide smashing at the stony beach. He felt more alone than ever. He could not understand that talk about orders and duty and responsibility. He could not understand his compassion for Hans. Hans would die and Oliver would survive. Might survive, as Hans had said. He wanted to pray to God to let them both—Oliver and Hans—survive.

Alex knelt in the snow.

11

Larry, wearing both his new mackinaw and high-top shoes, trousers tucked in at the tops, arrived as Alex was pouring shredded wheat into a bowl. He assured Alex he couldn't eat a single biscuit because he'd eaten so much last night at supper and then again this morning. But, without prodding from Alex, he indicated that he'd be willing to accept two pieces of toast and a glass of milk, because, he said, "I hate to see milk and bread go to waste." Toast, he said, was just cardboard without butter and jelly. He used a spoon instead of the available knife, so each layer was nearly as thick as the bread itself.

Ethyl and Harry Kellar were still in bed, and Lucy had gone to the café, so Larry and Alex had the kitchen to themselves.

"Well?" Larry said, pausing after he'd consumed his second slice of toast and dropped two more slices into the toaster. And refilled his milk glass.

Alex meant to honor last night's promise. He'd tell Larry everything. But sharing the problem did not seem so essential this morning. He regretted last night's performance and almost regretted his now embarrassing display of desperation. As of an hour ago, the world this morning was far different from last night's world. The change had occurred in about twenty seconds.

First of all, when he'd opened his eyes there had been the bright sun in a clear, blue sky. No snow, no

123

wind. Half asleep, with the sunlight through the window warming his face, he was just barely aware of the hum of conversation on the radio next to his bed. The voice, or voices, was continuing commentary on the latest advances in the Pacific against the Japanese navy and, in the jungles, against the Japanese army.

Alex had been aware of the war against the Japanese, but most of the time he'd ignored it. That war was twice as far from Pequod, Connecticut, as the war in Europe. The names of the various islands and battles were so alien as to be unpronounceable. Tarawa. Kwajalein. Eniwetok. They might as well have been craters on the moon.

Rome. Paris. London. Those were relatively familiar names, and their countries were actually the homelands of some of the families on his paper route. Several fishermen still spoke Portuguese or Spanish. His own great-grandparents had come from countries called England and Scotland. Larry's grandparents had come from France. Larry often referred to himself as *Franch*, a word coined by his father, and he had a dozen words that he swore were *Franch* but nobody could verify.

There he was, trying to slide back into sleep, trying to appreciate the warm sun but also separate the voices and the words into comprehensible messages, when, out of the mix of sounds, the word *Bastogne* leapt clear. The reporter's voice was exultant, almost shrill.

The reports have been confirmed. General Patton's forces penetrated the German lines and reached Bastogne. The siege is broken. The brave men of the One Hundred First Airborne Division have been liberated. Wounded American soldiers are at this very hour being evacuated to medical facilities in the rear lines and then to hospitals in England. Taking advantage of the clear weather over Belgium and Germany, Allied fighters and bombers are destroying German tanks and trucks. The German forces are in full retreat.

Entire battalions of German soldiers have been captured. The estimate of the number of prisoners is in the thousands. The final tally could exceed twenty or thirty thousand . . .

Alex leapt from his bed, intending to dash down the hall to his parents' bedroom, to wake them and share the news, but he decided to let them sleep.

One thing was certain. The Battle of the Bulge had ended. The 101st Airborne Division was already being honored by General Eisenhower. Oliver, if he hadn't been wounded, was now safe. If wounded, he'd been rushed to a hospital. Alex refused to consider the possibility of Oliver's having been killed. Lucy had vowed he'd be safe, he himself had willed it. He felt Oliver in his heart, in this house. Now, this morning, this moment, at this table with red-faced Larry Cobb chewing his toast and waiting for an explanation of Alex's strange behavior, Alex reassured him. No tricks. He wouldn't put him off any longer. But first he too needed toast and more milk, as if food would restore his trust in Larry's ability to help.

The Battle of the Bulge in Belgium had ended, but the ordeal in Pequod, Connecticut, continued. The German saboteurs, still determined to carry out what Hans had referred to as their mission, whatever that mission might be, were still free, still holding Rosie and Old Clara Kilroy hostage. The Germans could not take the women with them when they left the house to bomb or burn or kill or do whatever they were committed to do. They would be compelled, for their own protection, to kill the women, who, if left alive, would surely report them. It could happen this morning, it might already have happened.

In that sense nothing had changed. In spite of the bright sunrise and the success at Bastogne, Alex still faced the same dilemma.

Had they—Hans and Dieter—heard the news? Not that it would make much difference. They'd learned some of the details last night. But wouldn't it be fun to be there and watch the tall, skinny Dieter have to eat his words? American soldiers, he'd implied, were cowards. The Germans were courageous, inevitable victors. What was that song? *Germany over all?* Not at Bastogne, you stupid Dieter.

"Come on, Alex."

"OK, OK."

It was time.

Alex began by describing the evening he saw the face at the window in the Kilroy house and ended ten or fifteen minutes later with last night's farewell. Or at least with what Hans apparently had intended to be a farewell. "You know what I think?"

"What?"

"I think they're building a radio. They bought all kinds of things when I took them on the *Iris* . . . wire, tubes, dials, meters. That sort of stuff. I think they're sending secret messages. Or getting them."

Larry's lips formed the two words *secret* and *messages*. This was obviously proving to be more exciting than he'd expected.

Throughout Alex's telling of the story, Larry responded like one of those carnival snakes hypnotized by its handler's flute. He hung on every word. He even forgot to butter the toast and spread it with jelly. His glass of milk remained poised between the table and his lips.

Uneasy about misinterpretation, Alex delicately censored his descriptions of Hans. He couldn't admit to being so worried about a German spy. The dangers in Hans's sense of duty, as he'd called it last night, promised terrible, terrible things. Hans, and especially Dieter, were still *the enemy*, still agents of a country that just hours ago had been trying to kill his brother and any other American soldier they might reach. They were still spies, saboteurs, bombers, killers. The FBI was still hunting for them.

If Tony or any of the people at the café—men or women—were to know about their living at the Kilroy house, they would attack with rifles and shotguns and hammers and clubs and rocks before the FBI could be notified. The anger of the local fathers and mothers and brothers and sisters of soldiers already killed or still to be killed or already maimed or still to be maimed was not diluted by the German defeat at Bastogne.

"Why didn't you tell me the first day? We'd have figured something out. You remember that movie—I forget its name—about those spies? How the girl—"

"That was a movie. Movies are make-believe. This is real. Rosie and Old Clara could be killed if there's one little mistake. The FBI doesn't care about them, they want to capture the spies. If Rosie and Old Clara get in the way and get killed, well, that's just too bad."

"Hey, we have to help the FBI. If we don't, we're traitors."

"That's not true. I'm no traitor. I'm more patriotic than you. But . . ."

"Yeah?"

"Don't you understand? Rosie and Old Clara could be killed."

"So what? They're old. We have to stop those spies. Remember the pictures in the *Courier-Journal* and the stuff they wrote about us? We're heroes. Heroes are brave and patriotic and . . . Hey, what do you mean you're more patriotic than I am? Just because I don't have a brother in the army or navy doesn't mean I'm not patriotic."

"I didn't mean that. It's just that, well, Nazis wouldn't care about old women but Americans would." And Alex found himself wondering about Hans's declaration that he wouldn't hesitate to kill the women if he had to. Would he? Was he just talking to force Alex to give in, to continue keeping their hiding place secret? Hans was a Nazi. No, he was a German. He remembered those discussions when they'd tried to describe the enemy at school. Nazis are Germans, but Germans aren't necessarily Nazis. Something like Democrats or Republicans being Americans but Americans not necessarily being Democrats or Republicans.

"I still think we have to go tell the FBI right away, Alex."

"No. You promised you wouldn't tell."

"I didn't know what was happening."

"That doesn't matter. You promised. Heroes don't break promises. They always keep their word. Remember the Old Wrangler on the 'Tom Mix' show? 'Straight shooters always win. Lawbreakers always lose. It pays to shoot straight.' "

Larry was defeated by that reference to the cowboy who had been his great hero. He grumbled a bit and shifted in his chair but finally conceded. "OK. What do we do? Maybe they're bluffing. Maybe they won't kill Rosie and Old Clara."

"Who's going to call their bluff? Me? I *know* they're not bluffing."

"Your mom and dad are grown-ups. They know about these things. We're just kids. You oughta tell them."

"They don't know about Dieter. He's like one of those Nazis you see in movies. He's a fanatic. That's what he is."

"What's *fanatic* mean?"

"Sort of crazy. Nothing else is important but what he believes. He'd kill for it; he'd die for it."

Larry puzzled over that. "I don't get it. What's he believe that he'd die for? Me, I'd die if I didn't eat."

"I told you. He's a Nazi. He thinks Hitler's a god."

That did it. "He thinks Hitler's a god? Hey, he's dangerous, Alex. But the other one . . ."

"Hans."

"Yeah. Hans. He's a fantic too, ain't he?"

"Fanatic. He's, well, he's different."

"He's a Nazi, isn't he? He came here to blow up things and kill people, didn't he?"

Alex felt like a traitor saying it. "Yeah, I guess so." The confession sent shivers up and down his back. He didn't just *guess* so, he *knew* so.

"You have to tell your mom and dad," Larry said. "Or Lucy. Hey, Tony, let's tell Tony. My pap says no one ever messes with him, even with his one leg. Yeah, that's who we oughta tell."

Alex screamed, "Don't you see? I can't tell." He lowered his voice when he heard the water running in the pipes. His mother and father were awake. They'd be coming down to the kitchen in a few minutes. "You have to trust me, Larry. Promise me again you won't tell. Promise."

"It scares me. It's different than keeping the secret about the wallet."

"The wallet doesn't mean anything anymore. Keeping the secret does. Saving Rosie and Old Clara means something."

Larry's doubts filled his face. He shook his head. "The FBI. They're the ones."

Alex rushed into the living room, grabbed the family Bible off the radiator, and ran back into the kitchen. "Put your hand on the Bible."

"Why?"

"Just do it."

Larry touched the Bible but drew his hand back. "It's hot."

Alex grabbed his hand and held it against the black leather cover. "Swear."

"Swear? Not on the Bible."

"Promise."

"What do I promise?"

"Say, 'I promise on this Holy Bible I will never tell

129

a soul what Alex just told me. If I do may I rot in the flames of Hell forever and ever and ever.' "

Perspiration popped out on Larry's forehead and ran down his cheeks. His eyes pushed out big tears. "Hey, you're hurting my hand. OK, I promise . . . what? Say it again."

"Say it after me. No, no, keep your hand on the Bible. It doesn't work unless your hand's on the Bible. Say, 'I promise on this Holy Bible . . .' "

"I promise on this Holy Bible . . ."

"I will never tell a soul . . ."

"I will never tell a soul . . ."

"What Alex just told me."

"What Alex just told me."

"If I do tell . . ."

"If I do tell . . ."

"May I rot in the flames of Hell forever and ever and ever."

Alex refused to permit Larry to tug his hand free. At "rot in the flames of Hell forever and ever and ever" Larry trembled and almost wept. He finally completed the description of his fate should he perform the specified betrayal.

Alex tossed the *Courier-Journal* onto the upper landing of the Kilroy house after he had sworn Larry to secrecy. As Rosie had requested (what seemed now like months ago), Alex also delivered the *Boston Globe* and the *New York Times* . Then, after dark, he returned to the Kilroy house and hid in the shadows, watching the windows, creeping close to listen for voices, to make sure the two spies were still there. He did not leave until he was satisfied that Rosie was still alive. If she was, her mother had to be as well. He had not asked Larry to go with him. In fact, Larry had not appeared again after the ceremony in the kitchen.

Soon after Alex returned home, Rosie called the Kellars' house.

"Alex?"

"Yeah, Rosie. Are you OK?"

"Oh sure. But they want to know why you haven't been here."

"I thought Hans didn't want me to come again."

"Well, he told me to call."

He heard a man's voice in the background.

"Tomorrow, Alex. Please."

"I'll be there. But you're sure you're OK? And Clara too?"

"Yes, yes, we're both fine."

He tried to search her voice for signs of fear or pain, but her assurances seemed legitimate. No, not quite. Something was strange, but he couldn't say what.

"What do you do all day, Rosie?"

"Oh, we listen to our radio, Alex. I'm so glad Dieter fixed it. It's saved me from going loony. It's been broke so long I've almost forgot . . ."

Hans, in the background, said, "Enough rambling, Miss Rose. Finish the call."

"I'll be there tomorrow, Rosie, when I bring the papers." Before she could hang up, Alex murmured, "Rosie, if there's something new, something special I ought to know, just say, 'Fine, Alex.' If nothing's changed, say, 'Good night, Alex.'"

"Fine, Alex. We'll see you tomorrow."

In bed, Alex wondered about tomorrow. Whatever had changed would be important.

From comments made by Lucy and others at the General Store, he knew the so-called relatives of the Kilroys had taken the bus to New London twice since Christmas. Once they and Rosie, all bundled up in sweaters and coats, had returned with so many boxes they'd had to pay extra fare on the bus. They'd very liberally tipped the young man who drove them and their purchases home in Joe Critchlow's pickup truck.

What were they planning? They had to be planning something.

What *do* spies do? They blow up factories. They blow up bridges. They blow up train stations and naval bases. Those maps that had been found when the other spies had been captured . . . and those bus schedules and train schedules . . . *New London!*

They were planning to blow up the New London submarine base!

After that they would have to escape. Where would they go? How would they travel?

It was then Alex realized what had been strange about Rosie's voice. Not her voice but what she'd said. The radio. She'd gone on—rambled, as Hans had said— about the importance of the radio in her life. But Alex knew the radio *hadn't* been important. It had been broken down several times, for as long as five or six months. His father used to repair it but then no longer had the time.

What had she been trying to tell him?

"Rosie?"

"Yes. Why, hello, Alex. Hans and Dieter are upstairs. In the attic. Here's Hans now. Do you want to talk to Hans?"

"Say I just called to say I'll be late with the paper today. Before I get there, somehow, you have to write me a note. Tell me what you know. They'll be watching, but I have to get that note. Try, Rosie."

"I'll do that, Alex. I'll tell Momma you'll be late. It was very kind of you to call."

The stairs had been swept clear of snow. When he knocked and Rosie opened the door, Dieter shouted that she close it immediately. Before the door closed Alex saw Dieter, unshaven, wearing a soiled white shirt, sitting at the table, with maps spread out before him.

132

When Rosie opened the door again, Dieter was halfway up the stairs, the rolled maps under his arm.

Rosie took Alex's jacket and hung it on the rack near the door, then hurried into the kitchen as Hans came down the stairs.

Hans too was unshaven. He looked exhausted. His red eyes had to be giving him pain. Before he greeted Alex, he called upstairs, and he and Dieter spoke for several minutes in German. Then he came forward, indicating that Alex should sit at the table. He studied Alex's face, saying nothing but peering intently into Alex's eyes. "Whom have you informed?" he growled.

"No one. I promised."

"Promises," Dieter called down. "Such a gentleman. You are so honorable. We are to trust you because you promised. Young fool!"

Rosie, at the stove, was filling a plate with chunks of meat and potatoes and bread. She took the food into her mother's room. "It's about time," Clara said, each word sharp-edged, indignant.

When Dieter joined them at the table, he and Hans spoke in German again, each of them short and snappish. They were so intense and alert Alex feared that Rosie could not possibly get that note to him. They'd be observing her and him very closely.

"Your brother? Have you heard?"

"No. Nothing. My father says no news is good news."

"Your father is correct. Let us hope."

Hans seemed to be relaxing, softening. He was smiling lightly now, buoyed up, perhaps, by Alex's presence.

Rosie went in and out of Clara's room, in and out of the kitchen. She bumped into chairs, stumbled, fell against the coatrack, almost knocking it over, and complained about her fatigue.

Hans shook his head. He was losing his patience.

Then, smiling again at Alex, his composure returned. "There are no newspapers tomorrow. Correct?"

"Correct."

"Well, you will have to care for the old lady once more. Dieter and I will be leaving early. For most of the day. We shall return before dark. Rosie will be going with us. Just like the last time. Do you have problems with that arrangement?"

"No. That's fine. What time should I be here?"

"Nine o'clock is good for you?"

"I'll be here. But I better go home now."

Hans walked him to the door. In the cold, descending the stairs, Alex regretted that he and Rosie had not been close enough for her to slip him that note. What, he wondered, would be happening tomorrow? Rosie had looked so forlorn when Hans had described the plans for the next day. She could not take too much more of this. She was beginning to fall apart.

Tomorrow. He was sure that tomorrow would be their last day in Pequod. But what were their plans for Rosie and Clara? And for him?

Inside his house Alex removed his galoshes and leaned out to slam the snow off them. Then he removed his jacket. He heard a crinkling sound. In a side pocket was a piece of paper, folded. A page torn from an old blue-lined notebook.

I'm scared Alex. I don't know what's happening tomorrow. H & D upstairs a lot. They made a radio. Talk German in it. Sometimes someone else from far away, static, talking German. Twice a man came here. Once in a suit, once in a C. Guard uniform. Captain stripes on sleeve. Speaks perfect Eng. Also German. Upstairs once all 3 talk Germ. on radio. D. hit me yesterday. He & Hans argued. Hans hit him, shook him. I'm scared. Think they're leaving. I pray all the time. Momma's getting worse & worse. Please

The note was not finished.

Should he go to Larry's house and plead again for support? No, Larry would advise the same thing: call the FBI. He had to figure out something that would save Rosie and Old Clara even if it meant the spies escaped. Eventually they would be caught. The FBI always got their man.

But what would they do before they were caught?

He couldn't fill his head with so many thoughts and questions. The first objective was to save Rosie and Old Clara.

12

Alex knocked on the door and waited. Hans, wearing his wig, his short body almost lost in an oversize dress, opened the door. "Good. You will have breakfast with us? We leave in twenty minutes." He glanced at his wrist, at the thin, woman's watch. "Fifteen minutes."

Rosie and Dieter sat at the table. Old Clara's chair had been drawn to the edge, and she was gazing forlornly at a piece of toast smeared with jam.

"I've eaten," Alex said.

"You will have cocoa, won't you? Of course. It is especially good this morning." Hans poured the cocoa into a large mug and set the mug before Alex. After Alex let it stand, Hans urged him to taste it. Perhaps it needed more sugar. "It has vanilla in it this morning. Vanilla is an old Italian trick to make cocoa taste better."

Alex tilted the mug and pretended to drink. He let some of the cocoa skim his lips. "It's good. Very good."

"You are suspicious," Hans said. He laughed. "I don't blame you. Watch." He poured cocoa into a cup for himself and drank it down.

Rosie tried to be spirited, but she could not manage it. "He made Momma some biscuits. Crisp, the way she likes biscuits." She rattled on for a minute about Hans's talents as a cook until Dieter slammed his hand on the table and Hans, with a lift of a finger, drove them both into submissive silence.

Rosie's cheeks were heavily powdered. A new wool sweater was buttoned over an old turtleneck that Ethyl Kellar had given her last Christmas. She pushed Clara's plate closer and said, "Eat the sausages, Momma. And your eggs. Hans scrambled them with—" But she caught herself at what promised to be another flood of nervous chatter. When she stopped herself, she could not help but glance at Hans, who gave her a nod of commendation.

Old Clara pushed the plate away. "I don't like those things. They ain't eggs, they taste bad. I bet they're poison."

Could they be poisoned? Was that why Hans had tried to include him in their breakfast, so he could poison Alex? Of course, that was their plan.

"Either eat the eggs," Hans warned her, "or drink more coffee. Which will it be?"

"Coffee. I don't know where you get coffee these days, but it sure is bitter, the way you made it this morning. I like sweet stuff. Give me more sugar, Rose."

Hans, signaling Rosie to remain in her chair, dropped two more spoonfuls of sugar into Clara's cup. He waited while she tasted the hot liquid. She smacked her toothless gums and lips and drank half of it down. "Uh huh! That's better. I sure like sweet things."

Except for the coffee, the old woman refused to eat, even the slices of toast covered with jam. "I love ham," she said. "And bean soup. You never make ham or bean soup." She pounded her bony fists on her skinny shanks. "It ain't legal the way you don't make me soup. You know I love soup. I'll take you all to court. You're all under arrest."

Hans and Rosie giggled; even Dieter had to grin. The reaction only intensified Old Clara's frenzy. "Bang, bang," she shrieked, aiming a gnarled forefinger first at Dieter, then at Hans. "If I had a gun I'd make you dance, I'll tell you." She raised the toast halfway to her mouth, dropped it on her plate, and closed her eyes.

Her chin fell slowly onto her chest, and she began to snore.

Dieter rose and wheeled Clara into her bedroom. Rosie called, "Wait."

She went to a cupboard and returned with towels, which she spread on the bed sheet before Dieter laid Clara down. The two men went upstairs after Hans recommended the cocoa again.

Alex and Rosie had only enough time to exchange a few words. "That man was here . . . he's coming this morning . . . I don't know where . . ."

Dieter and then Hans each carried a small, heavy box from the attic and placed it near the door. Dieter took several strips of cloth into Clara's bedroom and quickly, efficiently, tied her while she slept. Then, in the kitchen, Dieter looked through the window. "He's here."

Rosie began weeping.

"Miss Rose, stop it. I told you we're coming back. You will see your mother this afternoon. Put on your coat and your boots. Hurry."

Hans looked like a middle-aged woman who might be a retired schoolteacher. He'd shaved his face and powdered it heavily. Rouge and lipstick coated his cheeks and mouth. A preposterous hat was pinned now to his wig, and a belt tightened the waist of his dress. He must have stuffed small pillows into the upper part, because he looked very much like a woman. His heavy wool coat looked new. It fitted him perfectly, as if it had been fashioned just for the shape of his counterfeit body.

Dieter, tall and slim, wearing ladies' flats and rubbers, actually looked more acceptable as a woman than he did as a man. A salesclerk? An office worker? His makeup had been applied with such precision that it was hard to locate the menacing face beneath it. Someone could mistake him (her) for a very efficient but loving wife and mother.

138

When Rosie dashed into her mother's room for a last farewell, Hans said, "She is convinced I am taking her out to kill her. Do you think that, Alex?"

Dieter, having carried one of the boxes to the car waiting on the road, returned for the second. He said, "Come, we're waiting."

Alex looked into Hans's eyes. "Are you?"

"You don't answer my question. Do you think we intend to kill the three of you?"

"Yes, I think so. But it wouldn't do any good. You'll be caught. You'll never get away."

Hans thought about that. "You have set a trap for us?" Then he held up a hand, interrupting any response Alex might have prepared. "No. Say nothing. I don't want you to lie. You do what you have to do, whatever that might be. And I, too. Sometime . . . soon, perhaps . . . we will see which succeeds. Whichever, you or I, I hope you understand I do what I must do."

Alex tried to translate the confusing information. As Rosie passed him, sniffling, Alex said, "You'll be back, Rosie. Do you think they'd leave your mother and me here, alive, if they weren't coming back?"

"Thank you," Hans said. He lifted a suitcase that had been stored behind a chair. "The usual reminder, Alex. We'll return in five or six hours. You cannot phone out, no one can phone in. If, when we return, I have reason to be suspicious, I'll have no choice. If there is the slightest sign that someone is near the house or inside, Rosie will be killed. Please be certain I mean that."

"I'm certain." In truth Alex was surprised by the unexpected conversion in Hans, who appeared now as he had the first day they'd met. Aloof. Professional. Alert to the demands of his job. He was not even slightly disturbed when the impatient Dieter, not too considerately, dragged the reluctant Rosie outside.

"A toast," Hans said. He poured the last of the cocoa into their two mugs. He lifted his own cup and drank. Alex emptied his cup. Perhaps, convinced that he trusted them, they would be kinder in some small way to Rosie.

At the window, Alex watched them cross the yard and go through the gate. Past the iron drum. Up the path toward the McCaffreys' house. Both Hans and Dieter supported Rosie, almost lifting her clear of the snow, as if she needed guidance to keep from falling. How loving they looked, should anyone but himself be observing. What considerate old aunts.

Alex had to go to another window to keep them in sight. A black limousine waited on the snow-packed road, white puffs streaming from its exhaust pipe. Hans opened the door and let Dieter enter first. Rosie was pulled inside after him. Hans closed the door and slipped into the front seat. The car eased along the road toward town, but before it began moving Alex saw, on the panel of the front door, in gold, the insignia of the United States Coast Guard.

Impossible. No Coast Guard officer would be a German spy. The man had to be someone posing as an officer. The car had to have been stolen. Or, like many other important items in this whole episode, the Coast Guard identification was fake. Phony. Counterfeit. Why?

Two threads this time. On the third and seventh steps. Which meant, Alex tried to convince himself, the men were honestly planning to return.

The upstairs room was neat, in order, as if its occupants had not yet arrived to put it in disarray. The closet—Watch it! Another thread!—had two heavy black suits on the horizontal pole, with bands of gold braid around the cuffs of the coat sleeves. On the shelf above the pole, two officers' caps, black, their peaks glossed with arcs of gold braid. Sailors called the gold decoration scrambled eggs. On the gold-braid medallions above the peaks: UNITED STATES COAST GUARD.

The dresser. Watch it! A single thread across the face of the middle drawer. Ease the end loose, remember exactly where it had been attached. Inside: a tidal chart, a line drawn under "January 1, 1945   1845 hours   + 2."

Tomorrow was January 1. Day, hour, tide conditions: they had to be meeting a boat. They would be getting something from it or taking something to it. Getting on it themselves?

Maps. Of Connecticut, of Massachusetts. Of New London (very detailed), showing streets, the entire submarine base (each building, each section, identified by name). A complex of buildings near the river circled in red. Beneath the maps: a sheet of paper containing columns of numbers. Under that sheet: several drawings of wiring diagrams.

The glue bottle sat on the desk. Alex used it to refix the threads on closet and drawer.

On the table, covered with a bed sheet—Two threads! Careful!—a radio. Actually a metal tray with tubes and wires and microphone wired into the Kilroys' old radio. Several pieces of what looked like radio equipment. Tools. A metal switch, flipped on, brought a red glow in midpanel and a hum, faint at first but growing louder. He turned off the switch. Could someone somewhere be waiting for that glow, that hum?

He reattached the threads, having a bit of difficulty now because his hands felt heavy, his fingers thick. He was suddenly very tired. When he descended the stairs he stumbled, almost striking the threads. Careful: the third and seventh steps. Third and seventh? Or sixth? He hugged the wall and stooped to peer closely at each surface of each step. There. To lift one foot and then the other above and over the thread required great effort, severe concentration.

His throat and mouth were parched. Excitement, he told himself. Tension. He lifted the cup that had held the cocoa. What had Hans said? There was more cocoa.

He should be sure to drink it. Yes, he wanted it very much now. But the stove was such a great distance from the table. Step after step brought him only inches closer.

They hadn't seemed concerned about him and Clara being left behind. Why? The radio, the uniforms: they obviously weren't worried about his finding them. They were sure of themselves, of him. He was at their mercy, that was why. He couldn't, wouldn't, do anything. He wouldn't sacrifice Rosie or her mother. They were right.

He finally reached the stove. So exhausted. The pot contained enough cocoa to fill his mug. The mug seemed as heavy as the pot. He bent his knees to sip from the mug, not trusting himself to carry it to the table. A bit too sweet, somewhat bitter. He straightened. What had been one mug expanded and receded, into two mugs and then one again. The single chair, as well, separated into two chairs. Then one again. The walls moved, rotated slowly. Faster. The sofa. In the distant living room. Maybe if he just napped for a minute. This foot . . . that foot . . . left . . . right . . . It must have taken hours, all day, a week, to travel from kitchen to sofa.

He stared at the ceiling. The house was cold. How long had he been lying here on the sofa? Inside his mouth, his tongue stuck to his palate. His lips, when he moistened them, tasted bitter. The drug they'd given him, as well as Clara, had put them to sleep. Why did they have to be sure this time that he would be in the house when they returned? You didn't have to be a wizard detective to know why. They wanted him and Rosie and Clara to be right here so, when they left, they could kill all three. That way they could go on and do what they had to do without worrying about betrayal.

Was he dreaming all this exotic mystery? These little games?

Someone had spoken. The voice had awakened him. He tried to rise, but his legs refused to obey. Someone nearby said, "They're back."

He rolled his head to the side. The voice came from the other side of the open door. Clara. "Clara?"

"Yes?"

"Are you all right?"

"I'm all right. They're back."

Finally at the window, he saw the black limousine. Rosie and Dieter were walking through the snow toward the house. Hans, standing at the car's front door, was talking to the driver. Then Hans turned and approached the house. The car moved on, sliding a bit, then disappearing.

Rosie pushed the door open and ran into her mother's room. Dieter came next, mumbling something about Alex still being asleep. Hans followed close behind. Neither of them would impress very many customers at the General Store with their femininity now. They wobbled on their shoes, their makeup had decayed and been badly restored, their wigs were awry, they swung their shoulders about like exhausted men looking for someplace to drop their bodies.

Alex pretended to be asleep. He watched them through slightly parted eyelids. He noticed Hans, sauntering into the kitchen, giving the cocoa pot a passing but close inspection. Dieter called down from the attic in German. Hans replied. Then he came to the sofa and shook Alex gently. When Alex continued sleeping, or pretended to, Hans shook him more vigorously. Alex opened his eyes. "Oh, I fell asleep. You're back. What time is it?"

"It is five o'clock, Alex. Come, you will have some dinner with us."

"I have to be home by six thirty. There's a party."

"By six thirty, Alex, Dieter and I will be out of your way. Relax, my friend. I will prepare a farewell dinner none of us shall ever forget."

"Except," Dieter said, laughing openly and heartily for the first time, "the old lady. She remembers nothing."

Hans actually appreciated Dieter's humor. "After dinner," Hans said, "if there is time, I will play Haydn. The *Emperor* Quartet again?"

"I'll stay downstairs," Dieter said. "I promise I will not sing."

They were acting like close friends who had just completed plans for a long, exotic vacation.

Alex remained on the sofa, tired, lethargic, his brain suggesting that he lie down again, just for a moment. He heard Rosie soothing her mother. Upstairs Dieter spoke German for about thirty seconds every two or three minutes, repeating the same phrase over and over. Once there came the sound Clara and Rosie had described. A voice from far away, covered with static. Someone on a boat was speaking German. Someone on a boat. Someone on a boat underwater. A submarine. Someone on a submarine.

13

If he was to live, Alex thought, he would be fifteen years old in five months. He would, by then, have known how to dance.

Angelina Bucher would have been his favorite. Now she would never know how he used to sit in class and watch her olive skin turn dusky in the sunlight filtered through the birch trees. She would never know how he sat for hours at his desk in Oliver's room, grinning at the invisible screen before him on which the movie played out his dream: Angelina accosted by some guy hidden behind bushes, and he, Alex, appearing by chance just in time to challenge the guy, to chase him off; Angelina, swimming in the ocean, caught by a freak undertow, screaming, pulled to safety by him, Alex, who had leapt into the waves from the deck of the *Iris* when he was on his way out to sea.

When Hans removed his untouched plate from the table, Alex looked at the clock. It was one minute after six. If six thirty was the magic hour, they would soon be dead.

"No need to wash dishes," Dieter said.

"No time either. Barrows—" and Hans, recognizing his slip, paused, seeming to anticipate some response in Alex. But Alex continued his apathetic daze. Slumped in the chair, still weak, he gave no indication that he even recognized Hans's presence in the room. He'd heard the name all right, and the name had

145

registered, but it did not provoke an alertness, a curiosity. Hans continued, replacing the specific name with an anonymous *he*. "He will be here in twenty-five minutes."

"You go ahead and change first," Dieter said. "I'll tend the fire."

Hans agreed and started up the stairs. Alex was sure that in Hans's mind he no longer existed, he was of no more importance now than Rosie or Old Clara. When the time came, his and their deaths would be of no more consequence than the death of a fly. As if he had sensed Alex's perception, Hans paused at the third or fourth step, bent low, and peered down at Alex, who was almost asleep. "Patience, Alex. I will try to explain before we leave. Don't be frightened. Distract yourself, go in and reassure Miss Rose. Old Clara is beyond reassurance, from you or anyone else, but go ahead. Talk to her." Then Hans continued upstairs. Dieter stoked the ashes and added more coal to the stove. He gauged the quality of the fire for a moment, then he too went upstairs. There the two men nonchalantly conversed in German.

They showed no concern now that he and Rosie were alone together, without one of them monitoring every word. Why should they be concerned? Neither he nor Rosie could do much to affect the Germans' plan or their own fates.

Alex thought about what Oliver had told him once about people freezing to death in snowstorms. How fatigue sets in and cold numbs the senses. They give in, lie down, and yield to sleep. Hours or days later, or in the spring when the snow thaws, the body is discovered.

This was how he felt now. So tired, so weak, so empty of will. The past days of near-defeat had taken their toll: he no longer cared. He would simply close his eyes now and let them do what they wished.

From deep within his apathy Alex knew that Old Clara was wide awake. His eyes were still open enough to permit him to see her sitting up straight in her wheelchair. And Rosie was neither weeping nor sniffling. She too must have made peace with whatever her fate was to be. Old Clara had not been so alert for a long time. She didn't say a word, but her posture, her eyes, her manner, made Rosie seem the older and weaker of the two women. Alex stirred. He heard Rosie's whisper, offered to the heated air of the house, expressing her own solemn acceptance of her fate. "They're going to kill us."

"How do you know?"

Silence for a moment. She had probably not been aware she had spoken her vision. She'd certainly not expected a responsive voice.

"I know. I just know."

"They?"

"Hans and Dieter. And the other one. The driver. He gave them uniforms."

"The driver? He had uniforms?"

"Yes. And papers."

"What papers?"

"In the car. That first time in the car he gave the driver the wallet."

The wallet. There it was. *The wallet.* Now Alex was completely awake.

"Where'd he get the wallet, Rosie?"

"From that old barrel. Where you put it. He was watching you that night. He saw you drop it in the barrel. Before Christmas. Today the driver showed Hans the wallet and some papers inside. Hans compared the papers, showed them to Dieter. Dieter laughed, said they were perfect."

"Did he say anything else?"

"No. He just said, 'You are a perfect George Barrows.' "

Barrows!

The name hung in the air, suspended, like a weight on a rope, swinging.

"We went right on the Coast Guard base. Right through the guards' gate. The driver showed his papers. Dieter and Hans showed theirs. They even had papers for me. I think I was their mother. Dieter's or maybe Hans's. The guard saluted and just waved us through. I wanted to scream, but I couldn't, I couldn't even talk." Aware now that she had been rambling, Rosie began to weep. Alex had to remind her severely to be quiet. "Alex, I'm so scared." She continued talking, but Alex was not hearing her, was not even listening to her.

Barrows. George H. Barrows. Back and forth, swinging: *George H. Barrows.* Then, as if the weight had struck his head, his mind buzzed and cleared.

Hans gave the driver the wallet . . .

The wallet. *George H. Barrows.*

The name on the Social Security card in the wallet of the dead man he and Larry had found. *George H. Barrows.*

Hans had watched him through the window that night, had seen him drop the wallet in the iron drum, had gone out and retrieved it. Needing a name for this other man, who must be a German spy as well, Hans had given the driver George H. Barrows's identity. The man had forged other papers to match those in the wallet.

Dieter said they were perfect.

So the man, whoever he was, wherever he'd come from, was now Commander or Lieutenant or Captain George H. Barrows. If they were ever stopped or if he, the driver, had to identify himself, he, they, were prepared.

"Your name, sir?" "Barrows, Captain George H. Barrows, United States Coast Guard." "May I see your papers, Captain?" "Certainly." "Ah, yes, fine, thank you, Captain Barrows. And your papers, gentlemen? Captain (Something). Captain (Something). Every-

148

thing's perfect. Thank you, gentlemen, thank you, Captain Barrows. You can proceed." "I hope you catch the villains." "We will, Captain Barrows, you can be sure of that."

"On the base. Did they go somewhere?"

"We went to several buildings. Dieter stayed with me, and we sat on chairs in an office, and Hans and the driver went off somewhere. They carried their bags. Heavy bags. Ones they brought from here. Oh, Alex, we can't do anything. I'm all cried out and scared out. Just let them get it over with. Poor Momma."

Rosie, you should have screamed when they drove through the guards' gate. You should have screamed, "These men are spies! Catch them!" You should have screamed.

Yes, she could have. Then the police would have captured the spies and come back to rescue Rosie and Clara and him and then . . .

But how could he be angry with Rosie? She had been as paralyzed by fear and despair as he had. No one could ever appreciate her terrified silence as much as he could. But he was not terrified now. And he would not be silent. He certainly would not be apathetic. He would fight back. Perhaps it was too late, but he would fight. His head was clear. He gave himself up to this new, intoxicating responsibility. He would do whatever he had to do.

"I'm going to run. If I can get outside—"

"The door's locked. I saw Hans lock it."

"Through the window. That's our only chance. They're going to kill me sooner or later. I'll jump. It will all be OK, Rosie."

Until now—with Dieter running up and down the stairs, carrying papers, maps, newspaper clippings, and feeding everything into the fire—until now they had been under casual observation. Hans, feeding a few last papers into the fire, was dressed in one of those two Coast Guard uniforms. "Hurry," he called to Dieter.

149

Dieter, upstairs, said he'd be there in a moment.

Hans draped his heavy greatcoat, the overcoat that naval officers wore, over a chair near the door. He balanced his cap, the beak covered with those scrambled eggs, on top of the coat. After some uncertainty, he lay the thin briefcase he'd been carrying on a chair, within the folds of the coat's sleeves. Dieter came down the stairs, a tall, slim officer of the United States Coast Guard. He had two full gold bands on his sleeve. His greatcoat was folded over his arm. He carried his cap.

Alex whispered a question to Rosie, but his voice was so low he had to whisper a second time. "When they left the base, did they still have that heavy bag?"

"It wasn't heavy then."

"How do you know?"

"Hans tossed it in the back. It fell on my lap. It was empty."

"Oh God, Rosie. Oh my God."

Hans chuckled. "Whispering sweet nothings to each other, you and Miss Rose?" He compared his wristwatch and Dieter's. "Ten minutes," he said.

"Momma!"

Rosie's scream alerted Hans and Dieter to the movement of Old Clara, who was rolling her wheelchair slowly, laboriously, toward the stove. She stopped when she entered an area of intense warmth and promptly dropped her chin to her skinny chest and began to snore.

"Eight minutes," Hans said.

Dieter nodded. "Exactly."

"In thirty seconds I will make the last call. You are prepared?" Dieter nodded and stepped aside to permit Hans to climb the stairs. Dieter, at the front door, looked out the window.

Hans spoke German upstairs, and there was a sharp, whistling sound and heavy radio static. Then a German voice from far away. Dieter went to the stove, opened the door, and piled several large lumps of coal inside, so many that the door wouldn't close. He placed more lumps on top of the stove, then turned the wooden box that held the coal upside down, spilling coal dust in several directions across the floor. The static died upstairs into an eerie silence, followed by the sound of wood and glass being smashed. Dieter did not so much as raise his eyes.

They were preparing the house for fire. Before they left they would either tie him and Rosie and Clara or shoot them and let them be consumed by the fire.

Now. He had to do it now. Alex took a deep breath. He would run and leap through the window when Hans was on his way down, while the two men were looking at each other, ignoring him. He concentrated on the nearest window, he bent his knees, prepared to run, to propel himself across the room and out the window head and shoulders first.

He heard Hans's steps on the stairs.

"Hey, Alex. You in there?"

A voice from the yard. Larry's voice.

"Alex . . ."

Dieter seemed unable to believe he'd heard a voice. He stared up the stairs, as if the sound had come from the radio.

Someone screamed.

The front door burst open.

Dieter reached under his coat, took two steps forward, pistol extended, but was knocked just a bit off balance by the presence of Hans's thick body. Tony—big, screaming, angry Tony, rushing as he had rushed before he'd lost his leg, when he'd been selected all-state fullback, rushing as if nothing else in the entire world could mean what this moment meant—big, screaming, angry Tony charged across the floor.

Dieter regained his balance and turned, still just a bit off balance, to face the charging Tony, the pistol swinging into position to fire. But Old Clara, who had pivoted her chair, practically threw herself and her

151

chair across the space and into Dieter's body, her feet and then her outstretched legs striking him just before, or just as, he fired his pistol.

Tony fell, rolled, stood, and hopped the final two steps to grab Dieter from the floor and hurl him as if he were no heavier than a football, or perhaps a good-sized cod. Dieter struck the table, which collapsed beneath him. Then he was on his knees, holding a carving knife. He tried to reach Tony, who had fallen to the floor again.

The doorway was suddenly filled with people, filled too with the words "Halt!" "FBI." "Watch out!" and the sounds of shots.

In the suddenly silent aftermath, Hans started down through the smoke on the stairway, saying, "I have no weapon, I have no weapon." Two of the FBI men approached Hans cautiously, then grabbed him and brought his arms behind him. They clicked the handcuffs in place.

A man at the door said, "It's OK, ma'am, you can come up."

Lucy ran up the snow-covered steps and in through the door. She saw Tony lying in a pool of what proved to be Dieter's blood. Tony was laughing. Lucy was crying. Tony said, "Gimme a hand. He put a slug through my wooden leg. Ripped it right out from under me. It's useless."

One of the men pointed a finger at Tony. "You're one lucky man, Buster. We moved the minute we got the call, but you were about a half minute ahead of us. You are one lucky man."

"There," Tony said, free from Lucy's arms and pointing at Dieter, "is one guy who was not so lucky. Him"—and he indicated the quite pale Hans—"he is also lucky he did not come down those stairs any farther."

Hans gave Alex, who was now caught up in Lucy's

arms, a weak smile. "Not so lucky," he said. He did not give Dieter's body so much as a passing glance.

"Can I come in now?"

Larry, in high-tops and mackinaw, the hood up over his head, his face not red but very white, stood in the doorway. Not fully in the doorway, though, mostly outside. His head and one shoulder were in the doorway. "Is it safe? Can I come in?"

Larry could not look directly at Alex when he said, "I had to tell, Alex. I had to. Do you think it will be forever and ever and ever?"

Before he was shoved into the backseat of the FBI car, Hans, his hands manacled, requested a last conversation, in private, with Alex. The agent in charge refused his appeal until Alex said, yes, he wanted to talk to Hans as well.

"Two minutes," the agent said. He and the other agents stood nearby in case the German tried to escape or to hurt the boy.

"Alex, I am glad it is over."

"You'd have shot me, wouldn't you?"

"I would have drugged you."

"Killed me."

Hans bowed his head.

"I wouldn't have done that to you," Alex said, "no matter what."

"Someday, when you grow up and serve your country—I hope you never have to, but if you do—you will understand." Looking about him at the growing crowd of police and the ambulance and the reporters, Hans shivered.

"Your overcoat's in the house. Do you want me to get it for you?"

Hans said yes, that would be very kind. "But why be kind to a man you hate?"

Why should Alex be yearning to run to Lucy, who was standing beside one of the two ambulances? She

153

was helping hold Tony up. Why should he be yearning even more desperately to run to his mother and father, who at that very instant were being brought to the scene in a police car, who stepped out of the car and searched the crowd for the baby of their family?

"Alex."

"Yeah? I'll get your coat." He ran as fast as he could across the yard and up the stairs . . . and into the house. He opened the draft on the stove, in an effort to cool the red-hot metal. When he returned and helped Hans place the coat around his shoulders, Hans said, "I will tell you, Alex. Not them but you. Perhaps it will prove something. There are three bombs. They are to explode in one hour. There is time." He identified three buildings at the New London base.

Afterword

As in most such stories on the page or on the silver screen, things turned out well. Fairly well.

The bombs were defused.

On the basis of Alex's information about the tidal charts, the FBI and the Coast Guard, convinced that there was to have been a rendezvous with a submarine in offshore waters, ordered a heavy patrol. Perhaps, attentive to the presence of overhead cruisers and cutters and patrol boats, the sub remained silent, far beneath the surface. No contact was ever made.

An intense search continued throughout the remaining four months of the war in Europe for the fugitive "George H. Barrows." He was never found. After the war ended and for many years after, Alex, as well as Oliver, were convinced Barrows was alive and well in Washington or New York. Perhaps he had become a wealthy businessman in Europe. Or a successful diplomat in Berlin. West or East Berlin. They could never decide.

In the autumn of 1945, five months after the war in Europe ended, eight months after Oliver was discharged from the hospital (and came home, as he said, "More or less in one piece"), while the slope leading down to the *Iris* (and to the *Esmeralda* docked alongside) was still green, Alex and Oliver spent most of each

155

afternoon and weekend fishing. In the spring of 1946, Dieter's remains were returned to his family in the village of Ibm, about seventy miles from Salzburg, in Austria.

Four years after the war ended, a week after Alex graduated from high school, he took a bus to Norfolk, Virginia.

In an exchange of letters over the previous year, he had arranged to meet Greta Stauffenberg (no relation, she volunteered, to the German officer who had tried to assassinate Adolf Hitler) in a hotel in Norfolk.

She brought her two children, Günther and Helga Maria, who, like Alex, were no longer children.

The four rode together to the federal prison to meet with Hans Stauffenberg, Greta's husband, the children's father, who was scheduled to be released in eight years but who, a new defense attorney was arguing, could be released in one or two. After all, Hans Stauffenberg had not killed a single American, and he had actually given evidence that had saved many American lives. A federal court judge in Virginia had already indicated interest and—an unnecessary and rare trait in federal courts—forgiveness. And—again, after all—the United States and West Germany were now allies.

Larry Cobb? He did not graduate from Pequod High School. He lost close to one hundred pounds and joined the United States Marines. Six months after he joined, he was promoted to corporal. Lucy and Tony were married by then, with two children, a girl and a boy. The boy was named Lawrence. The girl, Angelina. Ethyl and Harry Kellar practically lived on the *Esmeralda*.

One or another of the Kellars took the *Iris* out, out into the ocean, at least once a week. "She'll go on forever," Oliver said. He always laughed when Alex added, "Forever and ever and ever."